NATALYA SYANOVA

SOURDOUGH BAKING with KIDS

THE SCIENCE BEHIND BAKING BREAD LOAVES WITH YOUR ENTIRE FAMILY

FAIR WINDS

Brimming with creative inspiration, how-to projects, and useful information to enrich your everyday life, Quarto Knows is a favorite destination for those pursuing their interests and passions. Visit our site and dig deeper with our books into your area of interest: Quarto Creates, Quarto Cooks, Quarto Homes, Quarto Lives, Quarto Drives, Quarto Explores, Quarto Gifts, or Quarto Kids.

First Published in 2021 by Fair Winds Press, an imprint of The Quarto Group, 100 Cummings Center, Suite 265-D, Beverly, MA 01915, USA. T (978) 282-9590 F (978) 283-2742 QuartoKnows.com

Fair Winds Press titles are also available at discount for retail, wholesale, promotional, and bulk purchase. For details, contact the Special Sales Manager by email at specialsales@quarto.com or by mail at The Quarto Group, Attn: Special Sales Manager, 100 Cummings Center, Suite 265-D, Beverly, MA 01915, USA.

25 24 23 22 21   1 2 3 4 5

ISBN: 978-0-7603-7147-3

Digital edition published in 2021
eISBN: 978-0-7603-7148-0

Library of Congress Cataloging-in-Publication Data

Syanova, Natalya, author.
Sourdough baking with kids : the science behind baking bread loaves with the entire family / Natalya Syanova.
ISBN 9780760371473 | ISBN 9780760371480 (eISBN)
1. Sourdough bread. 2. Cooking (Sourdough) 3. Cooking (Cereals) 4. Grain. 5. Side dishes (Cooking)
LCC TX770.S66 S9 2021 (print) | LCC TX770.S66 (ebook) | DDC 641.81/5--dc23

LCCN 2021029161 (print) | LCCN 2021029162 (ebook)

Design: Debbie Berne
Cover Image: Haas and Haas Photography
Photography: Haas and Haas Photography except pages 5 (top), 7 (all), 8, 11, 16, 20, 36, 82, 88, 92, 94, 101, 102, 105, 106, 111, 113, 114, 119, 123, 126, 132, 148 are Shuttertock

Printed in China

To Sasha and Jacob
&
to every child
who wants to dive into a world
of sourdough baking.

· · ● · ·

One day you'll be ready
to start your own sourdough journey,
which will open incredible roads for you and
will guide you to new skills and
great opportunities.

CONTENTS

INTRODUCTION

Hi, my name is Natalya. My family and friends call me Natasha. And I love baking bread.

When I was growing up in Ukraine, my mom would send us to the grocery store every other day to buy freshly baked bread. I loved walking home with a warm loaf of bread and breaking off a piece of the fresh, delicious crust to chew along the way. After my husband and I moved to the United States, I tried to find the bread that reminded me of my childhood, but it wasn't available.

Once our kids were born, I felt a desperate need to develop healthy eating habits for them. The first thing I changed in our daily diet was bread. I wanted my kids to know what good bread tastes like and how delicious the crust can be. So, we don't buy bread anymore; we make it together at home.

Sourdough baking is a magical process. It slows down our busy lives and gives us a chance to go back in time to explore the roots and variations of breadmaking. The process takes time and deliberation, often spanning several days. But slow food is good food, and sourdough baking is a great way to connect with family and friends, enjoying delicious breakfasts, lunches, dinners, and treats.

In this book, you will learn how to bake bread using different ingredients and techniques. You will also learn the benefits of creating sourdough starter from scratch using only flour and water. There's a wide variety of recipes you can make with sourdough—from loaves to bagels to pretzels. I am so grateful for the opportunity to pass on my experience to you and your family, and to kids all over the world who will learn how to bring healthy, delicious bread to their table. Let's get started!

How to Read This Book

Some recipes require more time to complete than others, so be sure to plan ahead. The "Sample Schedule" included with each recipe should help guide you. Make sure you read the directions and measure all the ingredients before you start a recipe. This process will help you have a more successful baking experience.

Look for interesting facts about bread in the "Bread Crumbs" sidebars sprinkled throughout the book. The "Fun Part" of recipes offers tidbits appropriate for kids of all ages and the "Observe" sections highlight some of the science behind the recipes. Keep an eye out for parts of recipes that tell you to ask a parent or other trusted adult for help—these steps usually involve setting up equipment, using hot ingredients and equipment or sharp knives, or lifting beyond the capability of a child. I've included definitions of important words throughout the first three chapters. And, if you have a question about any of the words or concepts in the book, flip to chapter 3 to learn more.

WELCOME TO THE WORLD OF
BREAD BAKING

· · · • · ·

"Bread is the head of everything!" I remember these words from my childhood. Almost every person on the planet has at least one slice of bread every day and every country has at least one favorite type of bread. Italians love ciabatta; in Turkey, pita is very popular; in Mexico, tortillas are a favorite; in France, the baguette is everywhere; and in the United States, soft sandwich bread is a staple.

In this chapter, you will learn all about bread: what you need to get started, new words, safety rules of the kitchen, and the equipment and ingredients needed for sourdough bread baking.

Are you ready? Let's get started.

The Origin of Bread

Scientists believe that the first appearance of bread on Earth occurred more than 15,000 years ago. For a long time, people ate raw grains. Then they learned to rub them between stones to create cereals they then cooked. That's how the first millstone came to be, as well as the first flour.

The first bread wasn't supposed to be bread at all! Archaeologists suggest that, one day, while making grain porridge, some of it spilled out onto a hot stone and turned into a tortilla. With its pleasant smell, mouthwatering look, and delicious taste, this happy accident was the start of freshly baked bread.

Sourdough baking has an ancient history. About 6,000 years ago, people were learning how to break down grains into fermented drinks, which led to learning to bake bread through the leavening process (see more on page 12). This discovery, again, probably happened by accident. Eventually, someone developed a process that included saving a portion of the fermented grains and using it to "start" the fermentation of the next batch of bread. Since that time, humankind has been using "starter" to make sourdough bread.

Bread Science and Benefits

Bread is a great source of energy and many microelements. The most important nutritional value of bread is hidden in its slow (complex) carbohydrates. Unlike fast (simple) carbohydrates, these carbohydrates are full of healthy fiber. The body needs more time to digest the slow carbohydrates, so the feeling of fullness lasts longer. Bread contains protein—the main component of the body's tissues—that helps build muscle and keep the body in shape. Bread also contains a whole set of vitamins, including:

Copper, which produces collagen and maintains energy

Iron, which enriches the body with oxygen and improves metabolism

Vitamins B_1, B_2, B_3, which help the heart and stomach work and improve overall metabolism

Fermentation is the process that converts sugar and starch into simpler substances. During fermentation in baking, the **leavening** agent or yeast (sourdough starter) feeds on the sugar in the dough, which produces carbon dioxide (CO_2) that gets trapped in the dough. When the bread is baked, the carbon dioxide escapes, causing the dough to rise. Fermentation starts as soon as the leavening agent is added to the dough and continues until baking.

Vitamin E, which strengthens immunity, improves blood circulation, and maintains mood

Zinc, which improves brain function and vision and strengthens bones

Making sourdough bread yourself gives you a product that is so much healthier and tastier than bread you can buy at the grocery store. But the greatest benefits of sourdough breadmaking may very well be the enjoyment of the overall breadmaking process: It helps us slow down our busy lives, giving us a glimpse of what our ancestors' lives were like and the chance to feel, smell, and understand the dough.

Sourdough baking brings us into the kitchen and away from the technology that consumes every aspect of our lives. It provides an opportunity to reunite with our family by working together to make a delicious loaf of tangy, grainy, earthy bread completely from scratch using the most basic ingredients, then eating it together, talking about the experience, and enjoying that precious time. The process, however, requires some patience and discipline to achieve the best results.

To make bread, you only need four simple ingredients: flour, salt, water, and yeast.

Yeast is a living single-celled plant that eats sugar from the starch, releasing carbon dioxide (CO_2) and ethyl alcohol as it grows and reproduces.

Yeast Bread versus Sourdough Bread

There is a difference between bread made with yeast and naturally leavened bread made with sourdough starter. The main difference is that sourdough starter bread requires much more time to prepare. That sourdough flavor and texture are almost impossible to achieve with other leavening methods. Sourdough bread features a pleasing, crunchy crust, an open crumb (meaning the bread has air pockets and holes), a moderately dense texture, and a slightly sour flavor and aroma. Sourdough bread takes much longer to ferment and rise than other types of bread, but the result is worth it.

A **leavening agent** can be commercial yeast, wild yeast, baking soda, or baking powder, which is used to cause dough to rise from the release of gas, providing baked products with an open crumb and airy structure. Sourdough starter also acts as a leavening agent.

YEAST BREAD

Yeast is a single-celled organism belonging to the mushroom family. Airborne yeast thrives naturally on the surface of fruits, grains, and vegetables; in the air; and on the ground. Dough made with yeast—the method most commonly used by home cooks—is a closed system in which yeast cells live, feed, reproduce, and die. The speed of their reproduction depends on the temperature in the room and the amount of food (sugar) available. At high temperatures (80°F to 90°F, or 27°C to 32°C, and above), the reproduction rate of the yeast increases; at lower temperatures, it drops.

Yeast reproduces by cell division. One cell can divide twenty to twenty-five times, creating new cells with each division. The life expectancy of one generation of cells ranges from one to seven hours, depending on the environment and age of the mother cell. Yeast converts natural sugar from flour into alcohol and gas (carbon dioxide). That's how the fermentation process occurs. As a result, the bread gets an improved taste and aroma with plenty of volume and air inside. Commercial yeast was created to help bakers speed up the proofing stage during the breadmaking process.

Proofing is the process of the dough rising during fermentation.

Gluten is the general name for the protein found in wheat. It gives dough an elastic texture. The more protein in the flour, the better gluten development your dough will have during mixing. The dough will also be able to hold more water, making it much easier to work with.

SOURDOUGH BREAD

Sourdough starter can be created at home and can be used as a leavening agent for bread rising and baking. Sourdough starter is often simply created by combining flour and water, which is then fermented by airborne yeast. Sourdough culture produces a lot of lactic and acetic acids, which give sourdough bread its signature flavor. These acids create an environment that is too acidic for commercial baker's yeast to survive, so only natural yeast can live within it.

Sourdough breadmaking also makes gluten more digestible. The advantage of authentic sourdough for anyone with gluten sensitivity is that the lengthy fermentation process predigests the gluten, breaking down some of the indigestible proteins, and, literally, makes the bread easier for the stomach to process. It is also higher in vitamins, minerals, and antioxidants.

Equipment and Ingredients

Following is a list of the equipment, ingredients, tools, and utensils you will need to create sourdough starter and successfully bake the recipes in this book.

Equipment

- Baking trays, muffin tins, and rolling pin
- Cooling rack
- Dutch oven, or any iron pot, with a lid
- Jars for sourdough starter
  - 1 large (16-ounce, or 960 ml, or larger) jar for collecting sourdough starter discard—the portion of the starter removed before the next feeding
  - 1 small (8-ounce, or 240 ml) jar for everyday feedings
- Kitchen scale, for more accurate measurements
- Loaf pan (9 × 5 inches [23 × 13 cm] and 13 × 4 inches [33 × 10 cm])
- Measuring cups and spoons
- Mixer (a stand mixer is preferred), to make longer mixing times easier
- Mixing bowl (small, medium, and large sizes), for dough
- Oven mitts, for safety
- Parchment paper, for baking
- Plastic wrap, to cover the dough while proofing
- Proofing basket (called a banetton), or a loaf pan covered with a cotton kitchen towel
- Razor blade, or very sharp knife, to score bread (used only by adults)
- Rubber bands or lids, for the jars
- Scraper, or bench knife, to help shape dough
- Spoon, or small spatula, for mixing
- Spritzer bottle with water, to spray your hands or the work surface to prevent sticking while folding or stretching dough
- Square glass dish or plastic container (8 × 8 inches, or 20 × 20 cm, or larger), to monitor the dough rise during proofing
- Square or round baking dish to bake brownies or coffee cake

Ingredients

All bread is essentially made from four ingredients: flour, water, salt, and leavening agent (yeast or sourdough starter). Breads are considered "enriched" once other ingredients, such as eggs or butter, are incorporated. *For best results, bring all ingredients to room temperature before you start combining them.*

ESSENTIAL FLOURS

The type of flour you use has a huge impact on the final result of your baked goods. Sometimes, learning which is the correct flour to use requires a bit of trial and error. However, I mention specific flours to use in the recipes. Here are the types of flours that create beautiful breads. These flours should be available in your local supermarket; if you cannot find these flours in a store, look for them online.

All-purpose (AP) flour: This is the most common flour and it can be used in any kind of baking since it's literally all purpose. It has a lower protein content and can work great in cakes, cookies, or any savory baked goods. But it won't be as good in bread baking, which needs a sturdier flour.

Flour, a carbohydrate, is a finely milled product of wheat or other grain, or other foods, such as potato or corn; its molecules consist of hundreds of sugar molecules.

Purple corn flour, rye flour, or semolina flour: Used to add a unique combination of color and flavor to the bread or baked goods in this book.

Rice flour: Used for dusting a kitchen towel to prevent the dough from sticking to it.

Unbleached bread flour: This flour contains 12 percent or more protein and has a higher gluten content than other flours, which will help achieve a beautiful, open, airy crumb in your baked loaves.

Whole wheat, whole grain flour: Used to create sourdough starter and for sourdough bread baking. Choose stone-ground, whole wheat, whole grain flour, which will give you a much better result.

BUTTER

Butter comes salted and unsalted. Most bakers and chefs prefer to use unsalted butter so they can control the total amount of salt in a recipe. *In this book, I used unsalted butter.*

WATER

I always use filtered tap water in bread recipes. Water straight from the tap is full of chlorine, which might kill healthy bacteria or slow the fermentation process. Distilled water isn't a good choice either, because it doesn't contain the minerals that bacteria need to survive and reproduce. Filtered tap water has a lower amount of chlorine yet still contains all available minerals.

Safety Rules

Safety matters, and these safety rules will help keep you from being hurt or from getting anyone else hurt while baking in the kitchen.

To prevent messes or accidents, **ask an adult for permission before cooking** in the kitchen. An adult should also help you when working with knives or hot utensils and whenever you need to use the oven or stovetop.

Always **wash your hands** before cooking and eating. Germs spread fast and easily. They can even be in our bread and baked goods without us knowing it.

Wear an apron to protect your clothing. Also use a hairnet (if possible), or tie back your hair, to keep it out of the baked goods.

When using a stand mixer, **step away from the machine** because the ingredients could get onto your clothes or in your face, causing messes and, potentially, injuries, and stop the mixer, as needed, before you scrape down the sides of the bowl.

Clean as you go. If you spill something, wipe it up, so no one slips or falls.

Don't use metal utensils on pots and pans. If the metal utensil scratches the pot or pan, the scratches can leach toxic chemicals into the baked goods, even if you can't see them. Instead, use wooden spoons, or silicone spatulas even on non-stick pans—just in case.

Always **be careful when using knives** and ask an adult to help. Carry the knife with the tip facing down to the floor to avoid injury in case you slip and fall. You could hurt someone or yourself with a knife blade facing up. Also, wear shoes, so when you are carrying the knife point-down, you don't accidentally wipe out one of your toes if you drop it. Don't put knives or sharp objects blade-up into a sink full of water, as someone could reach in and get cut.

When working with a hot pot, **always stir away from yourself**. When lifting lids, lift them away from yourself, so any steam that may release does not burn you.

When scoring your breads, **ask an adult to help you use the bread-scoring tool**, which is very sharp, so no one gets hurt.

Always **put things into or take things out of the oven under adult supervision**, using oven mitts and/or a thick, dry towel. The mitts will prevent you from burning your hands. It is best to have an adult remove the hot baked goods from the oven. The pan, in particular, is super-hot, and we don't want you accidentally burning yourself. If you accidentally burn yourself, tell an adult immediately; keep the burn under cool water.

Check the oven and other kitchen appliances when you leave the kitchen to make sure they're turned off. You need to **turn the appliances off** to avoid a potential fire, where someone could get hurt.

Now that we know a little more about bread baking in general, and some specific safety rules to keep us safe in the kitchen, let's learn about making sourdough starter from scratch!

CREATING
SOURDOUGH STARTER
FROM SCRATCH

• • •

This is a very exciting, and also very important, chapter. It's exciting because, for the next ten days, we will create sourdough starter, a living thing made from two simple ingredients: flour and water. It's important because the process requires patience and responsibility to follow all the directions. Healthy starters increase your chances of success in sourdough bread baking.

The process of building a sourdough starter is magical. But don't be fooled—it can be tricky and downright stubborn. I'll teach you the habits of sourdough starter and its preferences for feedings, environment, and more. And then I'll guide you through keeping it healthy, storing it properly, and preparing it for baking. So let's dive into the science of breadmaking!

The surface of wheat and other grains is covered with many microorganisms that inevitably get into the flour. Once the flour is mixed with water, it turns into a very pleasant environment for all the microorganisms to grow, and if you give the mixture of flour and water some time to ferment, the microorganisms begin to multiply (reproduce).

So, what will happen over the next few days? All the microorganisms from the flour, air, and water get into the flour-and-water mixture and begin to reproduce. That's how spontaneous fermentation begins. Along with yeast and lactic acid bacteria, which we eventually need to isolate from the total amount of all the microorganisms, some bad bacteria also appear. Eventually, good bacteria overgrow and overpower this bad bacteria, which is why we don't need to worry if the starter develops a bad smell in the first few days. As the good bacteria overcome the bad bacteria, the starter will get stronger and more powerful.

A Note on Weighing Ingredients

One important key to successful sourdough bread baking is properly measuring ingredients. More specifically, measuring ingredients accurately and consistently. For example, not all flours weigh equally: 1 cup of all-purpose flour weighs 125 grams, but 1 cup of whole wheat, whole grain flour weights 120 grams. If flour is lightly scooped when measured, it weighs less than 1 cup of the same flour that is firmly scooped. As a result, it's important to follow the directions carefully and to measure your ingredients—including liquids—by weight.

Here's a step-by-step guide on how to use a food scale at home to weigh ingredients. In this example, we're making a loaf of bread that needs 2½ cups (300 g) of whole wheat, whole grain flour; ½ cup plus 2 tablespoons (150 g) of water; and ¼ cup (60 g) of sourdough starter.

Step 1. Place a mixing bowl on your scale and press the "zero" or "tare" button. This step will subtract the weight of your mixing bowl and set the scale's counter back to zero.

Step 2. Add the flour by spooning it into the bowl until it reaches the 300-gram mark on the scale.

Step 3. Press the "zero" or "tare" button again to set the scale back to zero, subtracting the weight of the flour and bowl.

Step 4. Slowly pour water into the bowl, with the flour, until the scale reaches the 150-gram mark.

Step 5. Press the "zero" or "tare" button again.

Step 6. Spoon sourdough starter into the bowl filled with water and flour until the scale reaches the 60-gram mark.

You have correctly weighed all the ingredients needed. How easy was that? Now, you are all set for baking.

Starter Process Chart

The following chart is a helpful visual of the day-by-day process of creating sourdough starter.

DAY	INSTRUCTION	NOTE
1	Create starter.	Let sit 24 hours.
2	Feed starter.	Let sit 24 hours.
3	Measure ripe starter. Feed ripe starter. Discard the remaining starter.	Let sit 24 hours.
4	Measure ripe starter. Feed ripe starter. Discard the remaining starter.	Let sit 24 hours.
5	Measure ripe starter. Feed ripe starter. Discard the remaining starter.	Let sit 24 hours.
6	Feed the starter twice a day—morning and evening. For the first feeding, measure ripe starter. Feed ripe starter. Discard the remaining starter. Repeat for the second feeding.	Let sit 12 hours between feedings.
7	Feed the starter twice a day—morning and evening. For the first feeding, measure ripe starter. Feed ripe starter. Discard the remaining starter. Repeat for the second feeding.	Let sit 12 hours between feedings.
8	Feed the starter twice a day—morning and evening. For the first feeding, measure ripe starter. Feed ripe starter. Discard the remaining starter. Repeat for the second feeding.	Let sit 12 hours between feedings.
9	Feed the starter twice a day—morning and evening—but with different proportions.	Let sit 12 hours between feedings.
10 and moving forward	Feed the starter twice a day—morning and evening—but with different proportions. Continue this process until you are ready to use the starter in a recipe.	Let sit 12 hours between feedings.

Before You Start Your Starter

A few things to keep in mind before you start prepping your starter.

- **Most important:** Decide whether you will measure your ingredients in volume (tablespoons/cups) or in weight (grams). The tables provided in each day's instructions contain both. Starting on Day 1, choose your measurement method and stick with it throughout the process. What is most critical is getting the proportions right in your jar.

- When you measure the flour, lightly spoon it into your measurement vessel—do not pack it in.

- You may need more water and/or flour on any given day for the starter to reach the right consistency.

* DAY 1 *

INGREDIENTS

	VOLUME	WEIGHT
Filtered water	2 tablespoons	30 grams
Whole wheat, whole grain flour	4 tablespoons	30 grams

In a small jar, stir together the water and flour. The mixture should have the consistency of sour cream.

If the mixture is too stiff, add a little more water; if it's too runny, add a little more flour.

Loosely cover the jar with plastic wrap or a lid. You want room for air to flow. If you use a lid, place it on top of the jar and turn it just enough so that the grooves catch. The lid should be quite loose.

Let sit at 76°F to 80°F (24.5°C to 27°C) for 24 hours near a sunny window or inside a turned-off gas oven, as the pilot light creates the perfect warm environment. If your oven is electric, you may have luck also putting your jar in the oven—just be sure to keep the oven light turned on. If your gas oven has an electric starter, also keep the light on inside.

OBSERVE

Don't expect much of a change in your starter on Day 1, except its smell and maybe a difference in color. Be very patient to let the bacteria work.

* DAY 2 *

INGREDIENTS

	VOLUME	WEIGHT
Filtered water	2 tablespoons	30 grams
Whole wheat, whole grain flour	4 tablespoons	30 grams

Stir the water and flour into your existing starter mixture, stirring well until you have a consistency like sour cream.

Loosely replace the lid and store the starter at 76°F to 80°F (24.5°C to 27°C) for 24 hours, near a sunny window or inside an oven with the oven light turned on.

OBSERVE

You'll see and smell activity in your jar today—bubbles, increased volume, and an unpleasant odor.

PROPORTIONS

I reference *proportions* a lot throughout this book, in both the recipes and in this day-by-day section. The proportions are specific to each recipe and/or day, so keep a close eye on the measurements I specify. I discuss proportions in further detail in the Preparing Your Sourdough Starter for Baking (see page 34).

* DAYS 3 THROUGH 5 *

Follow these directions, using the ingredients listed, for each new day, 3 through 5.

INGREDIENTS—PER DAY

	VOLUME	WEIGHT
Ripe (seed) starter (from what you created the previous day)	2 tablespoons	30 grams
Filtered water	2 tablespoons	30 grams
Whole wheat, whole grain flour	4 tablespoons	30 grams

Measure or weigh the appropriate amount of ripe (seed) starter from Days 1 and 2 into a new jar. Discard the remaining starter.

Stir in the water and flour, stirring well. Your mixture is now 1 part ripe (seed) starter, 1 part filtered water, and 1 part whole wheat, whole grain flour **by weight**.

Loosely replace the lid and store at 76°F to 80°F (24.5°C to 27°C) for 24 hours.

Repeat the process on Days 4 and 5, using the previous day's starter.

OBSERVE

On Days 3, 4, and 5, you might observe less activity—tiny bubbles, decreased volume, not as bad of a smell.

* DAY 6 *

On Day 6, you'll need to feed the starter twice—once in the morning and once in the evening.

Each feeding should follow the same 1 part starter to 1 part water to 1 part flour ratio, **by weight**, for the ingredients.

INGREDIENTS—MORNING

	VOLUME	WEIGHT
Ripe (seed) starter from Day 5	2 tablespoons	30 grams
Filtered water	2 tablespoons	30 grams
Whole wheat, whole grain flour	4 tablespoons	30 grams

INGREDIENTS—EVENING

	VOLUME	WEIGHT
Ripe (seed) starter from this morning	2 tablespoons	30 grams
Filtered water	2 tablespoons	30 grams
Whole wheat, whole grain flour	4 tablespoons	30 grams

In the morning: Separate the appropriate amount of ripe starter into a new jar. Discard the remaining starter.

Stir in the water and flour, stirring well to combine.

Loosely replace the lid and store at 76°F to 80°F (24.5°C to 27°C) for 12 hours.

In the evening: Repeat the morning steps, but for the starter, use the appropriate amount of starter from what you made in the morning. Add the water and flour, stirring well to combine.

Loosely replace the lid and store at 76°F to 80°F (24.5°C to 27°C) for 12 hours.

OBSERVE

Your starter is almost ready—it should smell better and be doubled in volume. But it is too immature yet to go into a dough, so let's continue feedings for a couple more days to make it stronger.

TROUBLESHOOTING

Active starter will rise in the jar in 4 to 6 hours, be full of air bubbles, and have a pleasant smell. But sometimes things can go wrong, so you may need to troubleshoot the problem to correct it. Here are a few troubleshooting moments you may encounter, with suggestions for correcting them.

No Activity

If there is no activity in your starter, something might be wrong. Unfortunately, it's hard to say what that might be. All starters vary due to environment, water composition, and even flour manufacturing or storage conditions. My suggestion is to start over: Perhaps try a different kind of flour (see page 13) or play around with the proportions of flour and water (see page 34) to see if this helps.

* DAYS 7 AND 8 *

Feed your starter twice a day as you did on Day 6, in the same proportions for each feeding: 1 part starter to 1 part water to 1 part flour ratio, **by weight**.

INGREDIENTS—MORNING

	VOLUME	WEIGHT
Ripe (seed) starter from Day 6	2 tablespoons	30 grams
Filtered water	2 tablespoons	30 grams
Whole wheat, whole grain flour	4 tablespoons	30 grams

INGREDIENTS—EVENING

	VOLUME	WEIGHT
Ripe (seed) starter from this morning	2 tablespoons	30 grams
Filtered water	2 tablespoons	30 grams
Whole wheat, whole grain flour	4 tablespoons	30 grams

On Day 7, in the morning: Separate the appropriate amount of ripe starter into a new jar. Discard the remaining starter.

Stir in the water and flour, stirring well to combine.

Loosely replace the lid and store at 76°F to 80°F (24.5°C to 27°C) for 12 hours.

On Day 7, in the evening: Repeat the morning steps, but for the starter, use the appropriate amount of starter from what you made in the morning. Add the water and flour, stirring well to combine.

On Day 8: Repeat the steps for Day 7.

OBSERVE

Your starter is now full of air bubbles, doubled or more in volume, and smells much better.

Liquid on the Surface
This liquid is a naturally occurring by-product known as "hooch," which indicates that it's a little past time to feed your starter and that your starter is weak. You can pour it off or stir it into your starter and carry on with the next feeding of flour and water.

Mold
Mold in your starter is not good—it is a sign your flour is stale or expired and that it contains mold spores. Replace it with new flour and start over, discarding the moldy starter.

Starter Overflowing the Jar
This is a very good sign. Just use a larger jar, or, at the next feeding, add slightly less flour and water. Continue to feed the starter twice a day with the proportions of 1 part starter to 2 parts water to 2 parts flour (by weight). Over the 12-hour period, it should reach a peak and start to fall. When the starter is falling, it means it is hungry and you have to feed it again.

* DAY 9 *

Your sourdough starter should be ready for baking, but let's make sure. And, if it needs more time to get stronger, you'll need to keep feeding it twice a day, but **with a different ratio of ingredients:** Reduce the starter amount by half and keep the water and flour amounts the same as you have been using; so, you'll use 1 part starter, 2 parts water, and 2 parts flour, **by weight**.

INGREDIENTS—MORNING

	VOLUME	WEIGHT
Ripe (seed) starter from Day 8	1 tablespoon	15 grams
Filtered water	2 tablespoons	30 grams
Whole wheat, whole grain flour	4 tablespoons	30 grams

INGREDIENTS—EVENING

	VOLUME	WEIGHT
Ripe (seed) starter from this morning	1 tablespoon	15 grams
Filtered water	2 tablespoons	30 grams
Whole wheat, whole grain flour	4 tablespoons	30 grams

To test your starter to make sure it's ready to use in bread, fill a medium-size bowl with room-temperature water.

Perform a float test: Drop 1 tablespoon (15 g) of starter into the bowl of water. If it floats, it's ready to use. If it doesn't, allow more time for the starter to ferment (ripen), feeding the starter twice today with the new proportion of ingredients. (For more on the float test, see page 156.)

In the morning: Separate the appropriate amount of ripe starter into a new jar. Discard the remaining starter.

Stir in the water and flour, stirring well to combine.

Loosely replace the lid and store at 76°F to 80°F (24.5°C to 27°C) for 12 hours.

In the evening: Repeat the morning steps, but for the starter, use the appropriate amount of starter from what you made in the morning. Add the water and flour, stirring well to combine.

Loosely replace the lid and store at 76°F to 80°F (24.5°C to 27°C) for 12 hours.

✳ DAY 10 ✳
AND GOING FORWARD

From now on, you have to feed your starter twice a day following the proportions 1 part starter to 2 parts water to 2 parts flour, **by weight**. You will feed your starter twice a day until you use it in a recipe.

INGREDIENTS—MORNING

	VOLUME	WEIGHT
Ripe (seed) starter from Day 9	1 tablespoon	15 grams
Filtered water	2 tablespoons	30 grams
Whole wheat, whole grain flour	4 tablespoons	30 grams

INGREDIENTS—EVENING

	VOLUME	WEIGHT
Ripe (seed) starter from this morning	1 tablespoon	15 grams
Filtered water	2 tablespoons	30 grams
Whole wheat, whole grain flour	4 tablespoons	30 grams

Continue checking the progress of your sourdough starter using the float test (see Day 9, page 24).

In the morning: Separate the appropriate amount of ripe starter into a new jar. Discard the rest. Stir in the water and flour until combined.

Loosely replace the lid and store at 76°F to 80°F (24.5°C to 27°C) for 12 hours.

In the evening: Repeat the morning steps, using the appropriate amount of starter from what you made this morning. Add the water and flour, stirring to combine.

Loosely replace the lid and store at 76°F to 80°F (24.5°C to 27°C) for 12 hours.

Importance of Temperature

Air temperature plays a very important role in the starter's behavior.

- In a colder environment (lower than 70°F, or 21°C), the fermentation process slows. Bacteria and wild yeast are less active and they need less food. So, you can keep feeding proportions lower.

- When the air temperature is warmer (higher than 70°F, or 21°C), the fermentation process happens faster, bacteria is growing faster, and the starter needs more food. Then, you'll have to increase the feeding proportions.

- Make sure you keep the starter at a temperature below 90°F (32°C) because a higher temperature will kill wild yeast and your starter will die.

For example, my sourdough starter is three years old. In summer, my kitchen is hot, so I feed the starter with 1:10:10 proportions (by weight). But, when winter comes, the temperature in my kitchen gets lower, so I feed the starter with lower proportions, 1:7:7 (by weight).

A young, immature starter requires less food in a 12-hour period. With time and regular, proper feedings, the starter becomes more mature and requires more food.

OBSERVE

Following, you can see how any change in temperature, feeding proportions, or feeding schedule delays or speeds up the process of ripening your starter.

The time frame indicates the beginning of the process as from mixing seed starter, water, and flour, until reaching the peak (double or more in volume).

PROPORTIONS BY WEIGHT*	TEMPERATURE	TIME TO PEAK
1:2:2	60°F to 70°F (15°C to 21°C)	7 to 10 hours
1:2:2	70°F to 75°F (21°C to 24°C)	4 to 6 hours
1:2:2	75°F to 80°F (24°C to 27°C)	4 to 5 hours
1:2:2	80°F to 85°F (27°C to 29°C)	3 to 4 hours

*SEED STARTER : FILTERED WATER : FLOUR

As you can see, the warmer the temperature, the faster your starter ferments as acids and wild yeast are produced faster, which makes your starter rise faster. On the other hand, the lower temperature delays the fermentation process.

If your house runs at a different temperature than what has been discussed in this section, you may have to make some changes to your starter proportions. I go more in depth on page 154, so flip there for more information.

CONGRATULATIONS!

You've now created your first sourdough starter—and it's full of life. With proper handling, patience, and care, sourdough starter can live many years. The oldest sourdough starter on record was 122 years old. Starter can be passed through generations and still create delicious bread. You'll know your starter is ready when it:

- doubles or more in volume 4 to 6 hours after feeding

- smells pleasantly sour

- deflates 3 to 4 hours before the next feeding

2-Day Starter Conversion

The following charts shows how whole wheat, whole grain starter turns into a regular flour starter in just two days.

DAY 1	MORNING		EVENING	
	VOLUME	WEIGHT	VOLUME	WEIGHT
Ripe (seed) starter	1 tablespoon	15 grams	1 tablespoon	15 grams
Filtered water	2 tablespoons	30 grams	2 tablespoons	30 grams
Bread flour	2 tablespoons	15 grams	2 tablespoons	15 grams
Whole wheat, whole grain flour	2 tablespoons	15 grams	2 tablespoons	15 grams
	Mix, cover, let rest for 12 hours.		Mix, cover, let rest for 12 hours.	

DAY 2	MORNING		EVENING	
	VOLUME	WEIGHT	VOLUME	WEIGHT
Ripe (seed) starter	1 tablespoon	15 grams	1 tablespoon	15 grams
Filtered water	2 tablespoons	30 grams	2 tablespoons	30 grams
Bread flour	3 tablespoons + 1 teaspoon	25 grams	3 tablespoons + 1 teaspoon	25 grams
Whole wheat, whole grain flour	2 teaspoons	5 grams	2 teaspoons	5 grams
	Mix, cover, let rest for 12 hours.		Mix, cover, let rest for 12 hours.	

Converting Whole Grain Starter into a Regular Flour Starter

While it's not mandatory, I believe that you can get better results with a regular flour starter, since whole grain starter is too heavy and too sour. But don't worry—you can convert the starter you just worked so hard to build into a regular unbleached white flour starter for use in many recipes. It's pretty easy and fast.

Different *lactic bacteria* dominate whole wheat, whole grain and regular wheat (bread) flour starter cultures. Feeding a starter with different flours undermines its health. So, to have a healthy starter, choose which starter to keep and which flour to use to continue to feed it.

I like a mix of regular bread flour and whole wheat, whole grain flour because the starter is then multipurpose. You can use it for white bread as well as for more grainy loaves.

Always choose unbleached bread flour and stone-ground whole wheat, whole grain flour for better results.

OBSERVE

What's happening during these two days? We are partially replacing the whole wheat, whole grain flour of the original starter with regular bread flour, and doing it slowly, so we do not disturb the army of microorganisms, bacteria, and wild yeast that has grown. Stone-ground whole wheat, whole grain flour is less processed and has more nutrients compared to regular all-purpose flour. This step will help us keep our starter as healthy as possible.

Caring for Your Sourdough Starter

You've made your starter and converted it for baking. Now, you'll learn important details about sourdough starter maintenance: how to continue to feed it, how to keep it happy, how to collect sourdough discard, and how to store it properly.

Feedings

Your starter is ready, but, like every living thing, sourdough starter needs food to stay alive. Your starter will grow after feedings and deflate when it's hungry. Your starter's activity is the key to making your bread beautiful.

Feeding your starter twice a day will keep it happy and healthy, and it will pay you back with delicious bread. We'll use a mix of regular bread flour and whole wheat, whole grain flour and filtered water for each feeding as we discussed on page 13.

FEEDING PROCESS

Twice a day, once in the morning and once in the evening, you'll feed your starter according to the amounts in the chart on page 25. *Important:* Stick with either the volume measurements or the weight measurements you opted for while making your original starter.

Pour water into a clean jar and add the active starter. Stir in the bread flour and whole wheat, whole grain flour until the mixture has a consistency of sour cream. Loosely cover the jar with a lid. It needs some air to breathe. Collect any leftover starter in a bigger jar, cover it, and refrigerate. This is your sourdough discard and you can use it for the recipes in chapters 5 and 6 (see pages 93 and 107).

OBSERVE

What's happening between feedings? After your starter is fed, the healthy bacteria and wild yeast from the seed starter eat the sugar from the flour and exhale carbon dioxide (CO_2), which produces air pockets and bubbles. The air bubbles show that the proportions of bacteria and yeast are multiplying, which makes the starter rise and grow in volume. It might double or triple in volume within 4 to 6 hours. After the starter reaches its peak, it will start to deflate because there's not much food left, as the bacteria ate it all. Starter gets hungry, overproducing acidity that makes it flat and creates liquid, so it's time to feed it again.

Note: If your starter gets hungry more than once in a 12-hour period, you'll have to increase proportions. Read more about hungry starter following.

Your Sourdough Starter Is Hungry

Every day, the sourdough starter becomes stronger and more active. One day, you might notice it's getting flat too fast, smells more sour than usual, or is not as bubbly as it was before. One reason for this could be that your sourdough starter is hungry. With time, your starter matures and gets older, and it needs more food.

Let's look at the wild yeast and bacteria that live in your starter in terms of generations. The more food you give them, the more generations can be created before they start to die off from lack of food. They don't really die off from "age" (of course, wild yeast can age as long as it has enough food to live and reproduce generations), but it dies very fast from lack of food.

Increasing the proportion of flour and water makes a big difference in how much yeast is created and how long it can survive before it either starts to die or becomes sleepy (this is the peak). So, if you only feed 1:1:1 or 1:2:2, and the starter peaks in a few hours, but you leave it for 12 hours, wild yeast will start to starve and die, losing its power.

So, to recap, increasing feeding ratios is a good way to keep your starter well fed, and adjusting your feeding schedule prevents it from peaking too early and becoming too acidic, hungry, and weak by the time you need it in the breadmaking process.

But beware: if you give the starter too much food by increasing the feeding ratio too sharply, it might cause changes in your starter's behavior. The starter will need to adjust to a huge amount of new food, and consume it, which takes more time. For example, don't expect your starter to peak fast if you jump from a 1:2:2 ratio to 1:10:10 immediately. It's important to increase the ratio gradually.

To understand whether your starter is ready for an increased feeding ratio, let's run a small test to determine whether your sourdough isn't getting enough food. Continue to feed the starter as usual. Here's what will happen in the next 4 to 6 hours.

OBSERVE

Happy, healthy starter will double (or more) in volume. It will reach its peak, then slowly start to deflate over the next 6 hours. A happy starter will be half deflated after 12 hours, smell fruity, and have a sour cream consistency. But a hungry starter will reach its peak in 4 to 6 hours and deflate over the next 2 to 3 hours. After 10 to 12 hours, a hungry starter will be very flat, liquid, and have a strong sour smell. If you notice signs of a hungry starter, increase the proportion of food you are giving the starter.

Hungry starter

Happy starter

When you started this project, you fed the sourdough starter with these proportions: 1 part starter to 2 parts water 2 to parts flour by weight (total ¼ cup, or 30 grams, flour):

	VOLUME	WEIGHT
Ripe (seed) starter	1 tablespoon	15 grams
Filtered water	2 tablespoons	30 grams
Bread flour	3 tablespoons + 1 teaspoon	25 grams
Whole wheat, whole grain flour	2 teaspoons	5 grams

Now that your sourdough starter is deflating faster because it's maturing and getting hungry faster, you need to increase the food proportions: 1 part starter to 3 parts water to 3 parts flour by weight (total 6 tablespoons, or 45 grams, flour):

	VOLUME	WEIGHT
Ripe (seed) starter	1 tablespoon	15 grams
Filtered water	3 tablespoons	45 grams
Bread flour	5 tablespoons + 1 teaspoon	40 grams
Whole wheat, whole grain flour	2 teaspoons	5 grams

Over the next 4 to 6 hours, you will notice changes in the sourdough starter's behavior. It will get happy, bubbly, and smelly (in a good way).

With each passing day or week, your sourdough becomes older and requires more food. If you notice changes in its behavior and it continues to be smelly and flat, you need to increase the amount of food and proportions again to 1:4:4 and 1:5:5. Higher proportions will help you stretch time between feedings, up to 12 hours, and leave your starter happy.

Collecting Sourdough Discard

People often ask if they can save a starter without discarding anything, simply by adding the required amount of flour and water at each feeding. The answer: it varies. In the early stages, you can fit in one jar:

	VOLUME	WEIGHT
Ripe (seed) starter	1 tablespoon	15 grams
Filtered water	2 tablespoons	30 grams
Whole wheat, whole grain flour	4 tablespoons	30 grams

In 10 to 12 hours, the jar will contain 5 tablespoons (75 g) of ripe starter. Without discarding anything, follow the proportions: 1 part starter, 2 parts flour, 2 parts water. So:

	VOLUME	WEIGHT
Ripe (seed) starter	5 tablespoons	75 grams
Filtered water	10 tablespoons	150 grams
Whole wheat, whole grain flour	1¼ cups (20 tablespoons)	150 grams

Tomorrow, you will have 25 tablespoons (a little more than 1½ cups, or 375 g) of ripe starter. By the end of the day, you will have 625 tablespoons (9,375 g) of ripe starter—that's about 39 cups.

Can you imagine how much flour and water is wasted by not keeping the amount of seed starter, flour, and water low, discarding leftovers, and using them for other recipes?

Here's a solution! To eliminate waste, every time you feed your sourdough, collect the leftover starter in a 16-ounce (480 ml) or larger jar. Label and keep the discard jar in the refrigerator. For future feedings, you will only use a small amount of the seed starter. All the leftovers should go into the discard jar. To measure the seed starter amount and eliminate the flour and water waste, I recommend you only take about 1 tablespoon (15 g) of seed starter at each feeding.

I usually collect the discard on weekdays. By Saturday and Sunday, there is enough discard to make Pancakes (page 115), or Blueberry Muffins (page 110) and Chocolate Chip Cookies (page 122).

Changing the Jar

It's not necessary to change the jar at every feeding, or even every day. You can safely feed your starter for the next 4 to 7 days without changing the jar. However, when the starter begins to smell, it is necessary to use a new jar. Scrape down as much starter from the sides of the jar as you can during each feeding, or simply wipe the sides of the jar with a paper towel.

I know life gets busy, and sometimes it is easier not to clean the jar for a week or so. When that happens, however, a crust of dead yeast and bacteria forms on the top and sides of the jar. A dirty jar can cause your sourdough starter to grow moldy.

Mold spores are everywhere—in the air, food, and flour. Your starter might have some mold spores, as well. Healthy microorganisms, however, like bacteria and yeast, can fight mold spores for a long time. But, once dead bacteria and yeast start to accumulate on the sides of the jar, mold wins and overpowers the healthy starter. There won't be any way back. All your hard work is wasted, and you will need to make another starter from scratch. So, make sure you take good care of your starter.

STARTERS CAN SLEEP!

If life gets busy, or if you're going away on vacation, and you can't pay proper attention to your starter—don't worry! Turn to page 155 for an easy way to put your starter to sleep and then wake it back up when you're ready to bake!

Preparing Your Sourdough Starter for Baking

Your starter needs to be at its peak of happiness and activity to help the dough rise and create a big, puffy, airy loaf of bread. To ensure your baking is a success, read all the recipe directions before making the dough.

The starter can be prepared the day of baking or overnight at room temperature. It depends on your schedule. I find it more convenient to prepare starter overnight on workdays (with bigger amounts of flour and water, or, in other words, higher proportions), so by the time I wake up, the starter has reached its peak and is ready to go into the dough. But, on weekends, when I have more time, the starter can be prepared 4 to 6 hours before mixing the dough, with smaller proportions of flour and water. If you prefer to prepare your sourdough starter 4 to 6 hours before preparing a bread recipe, follow the 1:2:2 proportion:

	VOLUME	WEIGHT
Ripe (seed) starter	2 tablespoons	30 grams
Filtered water	4 tablespoons	60 grams
Bread flour	6 tablespoons	45 grams
Whole wheat, whole grain flour	2 tablespoons	15 grams

If you want to prepare your starter overnight at room temperature, follow the 1:3:3 or 1:4:4 proportion, depending on the strength and activity of your starter. While 1:3:3 or 1:4:4 proportions are needed

for preparing the starter overnight, you can follow the handy chart at right for proportions referenced later in the recipes, too.

Combine your ingredients, mix well, and loosely cover with a lid so the starter can get air to breathe. Let ferment overnight at room temperature, and in the morning, your starter will be ready to use in baking.

Note: If you already have a starter and don't need to make one from scratch, or if the starter you made from this book matured enough and you are feeding it with different proportions, then stick to it. Just make sure to prepare enough sourdough starter for the dough.

OBSERVE

See how the starter doubles or more in volume, fills with bubbles, and smells fruity? That is how you know it's ready to go into the dough. Usually, I prefer to use starter as soon as it reaches its peak, before it starts to deflate. Use the required amount of ripe starter for the dough and keep leftovers of the ripe starter for future feedings.

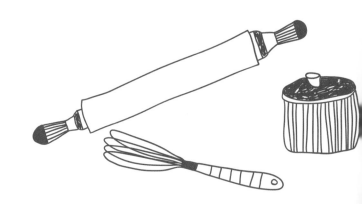

Starter Feeding Proportions

Proportions (by weight)	SEED STARTER		FILTERED WATER		FLOUR	
	VOLUME	WEIGHT	VOLUME	WEIGHT	VOLUME	WEIGHT
1:2:2	2 tablespoons	30 grams	4 tablespoons	60 grams	4 tablespoons (or ¼ cup)	60 grams
1:3:3	2 tablespoons	30 grams	6 tablespoons	90 grams	12 tablespoons (or ¾ cup)	90 grams
1:4:4	1 tablespoon	15 grams	4 tablespoons	60 grams	8 tablespoons (or ½ cup)	60 grams
1:5:5	1 tablespoon	15 grams	5 tablespoons	75 grams	10 tablespoons	75 grams
1:6:6	1 tablespoon	15 grams	6 tablespoons	90 grams	12 tablespoons (or ¾ cup)	90 grams

QUICK NOTE

Most recipes in this book require about 6 tablespoons (100 g) of active sourdough starter but be sure to read the notes within individual recipes.

STEP-BY-STEP
SOURDOUGH BAKING
CONCEPTS

· · ● · ·

Your starter is flourishing and you're ready to bake some delicious breads. Great job!

This chapter outlines the steps for sourdough bread baking, which I refer to throughout the book. Here, I continue to introduce words and concepts that will probably be new to you. Take your time reading the definitions and understanding the process before moving on to the recipes.

The 12 Steps of Bread Baking

Each recipe in this book requires essentially twelve steps from start to finish. If you've already built your starter and converted it for baking, then you've already completed the first two steps! It's best to familiarize yourself with each step before you start mixing and baking breads. But, of course, you can always refer back to this section if you have questions.

Step 1: Create the sourdough starter.
Before you can start sourdough bread baking, you have to create sourdough starter. (See pages 20 to 25.) If you already made sourdough starter, you have to bring it back to life (see page 155).

Step 2: Prepare the sourdough starter for baking.
See page 34. This is the same process as doing a regular feeding for your sourdough starter, but you'll need a bigger amount of starter than usual. I prefer to do this the night before I plan to make a dough.

Step 3: Autolyse.
Mix the recipe's called for amounts of flour and water until no dry bits of flour remain. Cover the bowl with a clean kitchen towel or plastic wrap to keep the mixture from drying out and let it rest for 1 hour. Some bakers incorporate starter at the autolyse stage, but I prefer to do it later because flour needs to get hydrated on its own; this way we get better gluten development and overall results.

> **Autolyse** is a simple process for mixing flour and water until no dry flour remains. Once mixed, let the mixture sit, covered, for 1 hour. During that time, magic happens. It may look like nothing is happening, but the dough will become smoother and more elastic. The flour will become fully hydrated and gluten starts to develop, which makes the kneading steps much easier.

THE WINDOWPANE TEST
After 1 hour of autolyse, you can perform the windowpane test, which will show you how hydrated the dough is and how developed the gluten is.

Wet your hands with water. Cut off a small piece of dough, about the size of a small plum. Hold the dough between your thumbs and index fingers. Gently spread your fingers and thumbs apart, slowly stretching the dough until it is thin and you can almost see through it, like a windowpane.

If you can stretch the dough without it breaking, that means the gluten is well developed and your dough is ready for the next steps. Return the dough to the larger batch and continue with the steps.

If the dough tears before you were able to stretch it, the gluten isn't quite ready. But don't worry. In the following steps, gluten will develop appropriately. You can apply the same test in steps 4 and 5.

THE WINDOWPANE TEST

Warm fermentation takes between 5 and 6 hours after the sourdough starter is added to the dough and best occurs between 72°F and 76°F (22°C and 24.5°C).

At a lower temperature (between 65°F and 71°F, or 18°C and 21°C), warm fermentation might take between 7 and 10 hours. At higher temperatures (between 78°F and 82°F, or 26°C and 28°C), warm fermentation might be complete in 3 to 4 hours.

Temperature is one of the most important aspects of sourdough baking (see page 26). You need to be aware of how long the dough should ferment at any given temperature. I note that in the recipes.

When yeast, water, and flour are mixed, enzymes in the flour break the carbohydrates into sugar. Yeast eats sugar, grows and multiplies, and releases gas and alcohol that are held by proteins formed during the mixing of the flour and water. This causes the dough to rise. Alcohol gives bread its smell and taste but, during baking, the alcohol and gas evaporate.

Step 4: Mix the ripe sourdough starter into the dough.

Using a stand mixer fitted with the dough hook attachment, mix the dough and sourdough starter on medium speed for about 1 minute, or simply use your hands to pinch and squeeze the dough until it comes together—do this for about 5 minutes. It will still be a lump but the dough will feel a little smoother.

Wet your hands with water and shape the dough in the bowl into a round. Cover the bowl and let the dough rest for 30 minutes at a temperature between 72°F and 76°F (22°C and 24.5°C).

As soon as the sourdough starter has been added to the dough, the wild yeast and bacteria start to work. The fermentation process (or warm fermentation) will begin and continue until the shaping process (step 9) and the cold fermentation process (step 10).

Step 5: Mix in the salt.

With the dough in the bowl of a stand mixer fitted with the dough hook attachment, add the salt. Mix on medium speed for about 3 minutes to incorporate the salt, or use your hands, kneading, pinching, and squeezing the dough until it comes together—do this for about 10 minutes.

At the end of mixing, the dough should be less sticky and more obedient. Shape the dough into a ball and place it in the bowl. Cover and let rest for

> **Kneading** is the process in dough making that involves incorporating flour, water, salt, and other ingredients until the texture is smooth and to provide strength to the final product.

30 minutes at room temperature (72°F to 76°F, or 22°C to 24.5°C, is preferred).

Note: You might be wondering why we didn't add the salt with the flour and water during autolyse. Salt tends to negatively affect gluten formation, so we want to give our gluten a chance to develop before adding the salt.

Step 6: Developing gluten strength and structure.

For the next 3 to 4 hours, depending on the temperature in your kitchen, the dough will go through warm fermentation. In other words, it will proof and rise. If you leave it untouched during that time, it will lose most of the strength developed during mixing and kneading, and result in flat dough without any structure. So we will perform stretches and folds, or coil folds, every 45 minutes. During that time, the dough should become puffy and grow by almost half its size.

Note: For all of the folding techniques that follow, remember that the preferred temperature for proofing is between 72°F and 76°F (22°C and 24.5°C).

LAMINATION

Lamination is a technique used to build the dough's strength and accelerate gluten development. The goal of this technique is to create elasticity, which results in a relatively open, airy bread crumb and springy bread texture. Lamination is best performed early in the warm proofing stage. It is also the best method for folding ingredients into dough, as we do often in the recipes found in this book.

To laminate dough, wet your hands with water and sprinkle your work surface with water. Place the dough on the wet surface. Start stretching the dough in all directions until it becomes very thin and you're almost able to see through it. Be gentle and try to avoid tearing the dough apart. This is the perfect moment to incorporate chocolate chips, herbs, nuts, spices, or any other flavors you want in your bread. Then, fold it back, as you would fold a blanket.

Sprinkle a large glass dish with water to prevent sticking and transfer the laminated dough to it. Cover the dough and let it proof for 45 minutes.

STRETCH AND FOLD

Stretches and folds is another technique to build gluten and dough strength. There are two ways to do this:

1. On a work surface: Wet your hands and sprinkle the work surface with water. Place the dough on the wet surface. Start stretching and pulling the dough in different directions. Lift it and turn it. You can have as much fun as you want. You should feel the dough become tense and less stretchy, which indicates there's enough strength in the dough. Next, fold and round the dough. Sprinkle a large glass dish with water to prevent sticking and transfer the stretched dough to it. Cover the dough and let it proof for 45 minutes.

2. In the bowl: Wet your hands with water and start stretching and pulling the dough in different directions in the bowl. Lift and turn it under so

the smooth surface remains on top. You should feel the dough become tense and less stretchy. Fold and round the dough, cover, and let proof for 45 minutes.

COIL FOLD

Coil folding is another method of strengthening and developing the gluten in dough. It's better to use a square or rectangular container for coil folds, as it will lend to the symmetrical motion of coil folding.

- Sprinkle your hands with water and pick up the dough from the middle. Lift it, allowing it to stretch until one end releases from the proofing container.

- Then, lower the dough to tuck the loose end under the middle.

- Repeat this process for the other end.

- With the dough in the container, rotate the container 90 degrees and repeat the process until the dough holds its shape.

By the end of the stretching, the dough becomes more pliable, airy, and much easier to handle. It should grow by about 50 percent in volume. Sometimes, warm fermentation requires one extra stretch; this depends on the temperature in your kitchen or the strength of your starter. After the final stretch, cover the dough and let it rest for its final proof for 30 to 45 minutes.

Coil fold: Lift the dough so it stretches and pulls away from the container.

Coil fold: Tuck the loose end under.

Step 7: Final proof.

During this stage, let the dough rise untouched. There is no exact time to end warm fermentation and it requires some practice to know when to do so. With time, you'll learn to read the dough's strength, elasticity, tension, volume, and amount of air inside. The length of the final proof depends on the temperature of the environment, the strength of your starter, and how the dough reacts to all the manipulations. The final proof should take 30 minutes to 1 hour. By the end of the final proof, the dough grows about 50 percent in volume.

If warm fermentation went well, the dough will be very light and have a bouncy feel to it. If you gently move the bowl or container back and forth, the dough will jiggle. Look for the following visual cues to know when the proof is sufficient:

- 50 percent increase in volume

- Bubbles beneath the surface of the dough or along the sides of the bowl

- Domed shape, indicating the dough is still growing and has strength left in it

- Smooth, shiny surface

If you end warm fermentation too early, your dough will be *underproofed*, resulting in a flat, pale, gummy loaf of bread. Conversely, if you push warm fermentation too far, your dough will be *overproofed*, resulting in sticky, hard-to-handle dough that won't open during baking.

When you first put the dough in the glass dish, there may be space on either side of it . . . but after the dough has sufficiently proofed, you'll see it takes up the entire area!

Step 8: Preshape the dough.

If your dough feels a little loose, you can give it a slightly tighter preshape. Some bakers skip the preshape step, but I prefer to do it. It's the last point when you can organize and add some structure and strength to the dough that might otherwise be tricky to shape. During preshaping, the dough needs to be handled very gently so as not to deflate the air pockets that developed during warm fermentation, as these air pockets will create the open crumb, or interior structure, of the bread after it's baked.

To preshape the dough, sprinkle your work surface with some flour and turn the bowl containing the dough upside down, so the dough releases itself. If the dough is proofed properly and gains enough strength during the warm fermentation process, it will release from the glass dish by itself. The smooth side of the dough needs to be on the bottom.

Note: If the dough won't release from the glass dish by itself, you can wet your hands and help it break free from the bowl or use a scraper or spatula.

Working to keep as much air in the dough as possible, pull the dough up from the middle and tuck the dough around itself. Using a bench scraper, flip the dough upside down. Now, the smooth, floured surface will be on top. Gently round the loaf with your hands and let it rest, uncovered, for 30 minutes. The dough should keep its shape but may relax (or spread) a little.

If the dough is over- or underproofed, it will spread without holding any shape after 30 minutes of preshaping. If that's the case, give it another preshape and let it rest for 20 minutes more before proceeding to step 9.

Step 9: Shaping the dough.

To shape the dough, dust the top of the preshaped dough with flour. Use a dough scraper or bench knife to flip the dough over onto a work surface, so the floured side is down. The two most common loaf shapes are oval (batard) and round (boule). Follow the instructions and photos at right to shape your dough.

Note: The bottom of the dough, which rests on the work surface, is usually uneven and bumpy, while the top surface of the dough is usually smooth. You want the smooth surface to become the outside, or top, of the loaf. So, when shaping the dough, place the smooth side against the work surface. As you shape the dough, the smooth surface will grip the work surface slightly, helping create a better, final shape.

When your dough is shaped, transfer the roll, seam-side up, to a prepared proofing basket (or a loaf pan lined with a kitchen towel sprinkled with rice flour to prevent sticking). Cover the dough with plastic wrap and return the dough to the 72°F to 76°F (22°C to 24.5°C) environment for 15 minutes. Then, transfer the dough, covered, to the refrigerator (preferred temperature 40°F, or 4°C) to slow rise (retard) for at least 8 to 14 hours (enough time for the loaf to slowly ferment at a lower temperature), but try not to keep the dough in the refrigerator more than 24 hours, otherwise your loaf will get too tangy.

Step 10: Retard, or cold fermentation.

In breadmaking, retarding is a technique that slows the fermentation process of your dough. After the dough has been shaped and rested for 15 minutes, transfer it, covered, to the refrigerator for cold fermentation for 8 to 24 hours.

This slower process gives you the flexibility to bake your loaves at a later time. For instance, if you want freshly baked bread in the morning, you can

OVAL (BATARD)-SHAPED LOAF

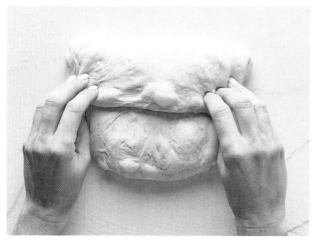

Starting with the side closest to you, pull the right two corners of the dough to the left, then fold them up into half the dough. Repeat this action with the other side.

Finally, roll the dough. Shape it into a smooth, taut roll and pinch the sides to seal them.

ROUND (BOULE)-SHAPED LOAF

Pull the edges of the dough toward the center four or five times, working around the circumference of the dough. Gather and pinch together the corners of the folds to form a sack shape.

Flip the dough upside down so the pinched corners are on the bottom. Gently tuck the pinched corners underneath the dough round and return it to an upright position.

schedule your bread baking accordingly by letting your shaped loaves proof slowly in the refrigerator overnight. When you are ready to bake, you can simply take them out of the refrigerator as soon as your oven is hot enough. In other words, it's a slow, cold fermentation, which not only makes bread baking more convenient, but also slows the yeast development in the cooler temperatures. During that time, bacteria produce lactic and acetic acids, giving your bread more flavor.

A loaf treated with a cold retard is the best way to achieve an extremely light, airy crumb. Every cell in the loaf has a chance to accumulate the maximum amount of gas. When the loaf goes into the oven, all that cold gas expands and blows up, which is what creates that wonderfully open structure.

Note: An adult should perform all the actions in these steps while you observe the process.

Step 11: Scoring.

One hour before baking, place an empty cast-iron pan, or a Dutch oven with a lid, into a cold oven. Preheat the oven to 500°F (250°F) and let it heat for 1 hour. The oven should be very hot to create the effect of the professional ovens used in bakeries.

Once the oven is hot, place a sheet of parchment paper on a cutting board. Remove the cold dough from the refrigerator and flip it onto the parchment paper. The smooth part of the dough should be on top, and the sealed part should rest on the parchment. Next, an adult should score the bread.

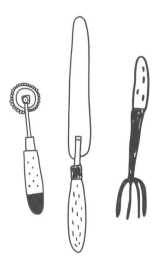

Scoring prepares the loaf for fast expansion in the hot oven. When yeast enters a very hot environment, it quickly evaporates carbon dioxide (CO_2) gas, which leads to a fast rise and blooming bread. To score bread, slash the top of the loaf at a 45-degree angle with a blade, or a sharp knife, about ½ inch (1 cm) deeper than the outer surface (or below any outer coating). Some bakers like to make one long slash whereas others prefer many smaller slashes. The purpose is to control the direction in which the bread rises during baking and the bread's ability to expand. Bread that isn't scored may open in unexpected places during the baking process.

Wet a very sharp blade with water between scorings, especially when working with sticky dough. Let the blade do the hard work. Don't press down on the dough. Much like cutting paper with a knife, where, upon finding the perfect angle, the blade will run through paper smoothly without ripping it, the same applies to dough. With practice, you'll be able to feel the correct angle and run the blade smoothly through the dough and discover what works best for you.

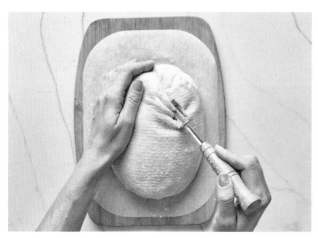

SCORING AN OVAL (BATARD) LOAF
To create an "ear" (a portion of raised crust), hold the knife blade at a shallow angle (about 45 degrees) to the surface of the loaf and make a slash about ½ inch (1 cm) deep. Again, you can make either one long slash or many smaller slashes. It is up to you.

SCORING A ROUND (BOULE) LOAF
There are unlimited design possibilities to score round loaves. Before you score the dough, sprinkle some white rice flour on top of the loaf (use a sifter for a more even application). This helps show maximum contrast between the white flour and the dark baked crust. With an adult helper using a very sharp blade and your imagination guiding the process, score the dough (again, ½ inch, or 1 cm, deep is optimal)—consider a crosscut, square cut, many small cuts, or even a smiley face.

Step 12: Baking.

The breads in this book will be baked in a Dutch oven or other iron pot with a lid. After the Dutch oven is preheated, as described in step 11, your adult helper, wearing oven mitts, should remove the hot pan from the oven. Wearing oven mitts, pick up the cutting board with the scored loaf on it in one hand and carefully pull the parchment paper toward the hot pan with your other hand. Slide the dough and parchment into the pan and cover the pan with a lid. Transfer the pan to the oven and bake the dough for 15 minutes.

After the first 15 minutes of baking, remove the lid and lower the oven temperature to 450°F (230°C). Bake the bread for 20 to 25 minutes, or until it's dark golden brown. When the loaf is ready, remove it from the hot oven. Carefully use the parchment paper to lift the loaf out of the hot Dutch oven and place it on a cooling rack to cool for 1 hour.

OBSERVE

What happens to the dough while it bakes? A very hot Dutch oven, or cast-iron pan, with a lid, traps the steam from the dough inside the cooking vessel, keeping the surface of the loaf moist while it bakes. Moist air inside the pot allows the surface of the dough to expand and develop a crisp, shiny crust. Once the loaf has risen fully, remove the lid and let the steam evaporate, then continue baking in a dry (not steamy) hot oven. If you continue baking with steam the whole time, the crust becomes thick and rubbery.

Butter-Enriched Sourdough Loaf
page 56

CHAPTER 4

RECIPES
WITH SOURDOUGH STARTER

• • • •

In this chapter, we'll do some sourdough bread baking with many healthy recipes. You'll learn how simple the sourdough bread baking process can be when you follow the directions carefully. We will turn a simple sourdough bread into a burst of colors and flavors. We will use different ingredients and techniques and observe the science behind the sourdough breadmaking process.

Basic Sourdough Loaf

10 to 12 slices

This is a straightforward sourdough bread formula that every young baker can make. Prepare the sourdough starter the night before, so you'll be able to work on the dough first thing in the morning. This was one of the first recipes I tried when I was learning to bake sourdough bread.

SOURDOUGH STARTER
Ripe (seed) starter:
2 tablespoons | 30 grams

Filtered water:
½ cup | 120 grams

Bread flour:
14 tablespoons | 105 grams

Whole wheat, whole
grain flour:
2 tablespoons | 15 grams

DOUGH
600 g bread flour, or add more flavor to the loaf by mixing 500 g bread flour with 100 g whole wheat, whole grain flour

400 g filtered water (add 25 to 30 g water for the whole wheat, whole grain flour option)

200 g sourdough starter

12 g salt

To make the sourdough starter: In a jar, stir together all the starter ingredients and loosely cover the jar. Let the starter ferment at room temperature overnight to reach its peak. It will double or more in volume by morning.

To make the dough: When the starter is ready, ask an adult to set up a stand mixer fitted with the dough hook attachment. Add the flour and water to the bowl and mix on low speed for 1 minute. Cover the bowl and let soak for 1 hour to autolyse (see page 38).

Add the sourdough starter to the dough and mix on medium speed for 1 to 2 minutes. Cover and let rest for 30 minutes.

Add the salt and mix on medium speed for 2 to 4 minutes.

Observe
By the end of mixing, the dough should hold together and clear the sides of the bowl, but still stick to the bottom.

Round the dough with wet hands. Cover and let rest for 30 minutes.

Fun Part
Perform the first stretch on a wet work surface or in the bowl (read more on page 40).

Sprinkle a square glass dish or container with water to prevent sticking and transfer the dough to it. Cover and let rest for 45 minutes.

Perform 3 more coil folds or stretch and folds (see page 42 or 40), each 45 minutes apart.

CONTINUED

BREADCRUMBS

While they mean the same thing, the term "sourdough starter" is more popular in the United States and "levain" is more popular in France.

Observe

With each folding, you will be able to feel and see how the dough gets stronger, less sticky, airy, puffy, and easier to work with.

After the final stretch, leave the dough untouched for 30 minutes for the final proof before preshaping.

Preshape the dough and let it rest, uncovered, for 30 minutes (read more on page 43).

Shape the dough (see page 44), then transfer it to a proofing basket, cover, and let proof for 2 hours at room temperature. Then, refrigerate the dough for 2 to 4 hours. This helps harden the crust and makes scoring the loaf easier.

An adult should perform all the actions in these steps while you observe the process. Place a Dutch oven in the oven and preheat the oven to 500°F (250°C). Let the oven heat for 45 minutes.

When the oven is hot, ask an adult to remove the hot pot from the oven. Remove the dough from the refrigerator and flip it onto a piece of parchment paper. Ask an adult helper to score the loaf and transfer it to the hot Dutch oven. Put the lid on the Dutch oven and bake the dough for 15 minutes. Ask an adult to remove the hot lid. Lower the oven temperature to 450°F (230°C) and bake the loaf for 25 minutes more until golden brown.

Ask a parent or other trusted adult to remove the hot pot from the oven and then use the parchment paper to lift the loaf out of the hot Dutch oven and place it on a cooling rack. Let cool for 1 to 2 hours and enjoy.

Sample Schedule

After an overnight rest for the starter, you'll need about 10 hours to complete this recipe.

	DAY 1	DAY 2
Mix the starter ingredients	6:00 p.m.	
Soak the water and flour		8:00 a.m.
Add the starter		9:00 a.m.
Add salt and shape the dough		9:30 a.m.
Stretch 1		10:00 a.m.
Stretch/fold 2		10:45 a.m.
Stretch/fold 3		11:30 a.m.
Stretch/fold 4		12:15 p.m.
Preshape		12:45 p.m.
Shape and proof		1:15 p.m.
Refrigerate		3:15 p.m.
Preheat Dutch oven		4:30 p.m.
Bake		5:15 p.m.

Country-Style Sourdough Bread

10 to 12 slices

400 g bread flour

75 g whole wheat, whole grain flour

25 g rye flour

390 g filtered water

100 g active sourdough starter (see page 34)

10 g salt

If you like a crusty open-crumb loaf full of tangy flavor, blisters outside and holes inside, then this recipe is for you. Be patient and prepared; feed your starter well because the nature of bread baking at home is unpredictable. Much depends on the strength of your starter, the temperature in the kitchen, and the time you spend on each step—all of which affect the result.

Ask an adult to set up a stand mixer fitted with the dough hook attachment. Add the flours and water to the bowl and mix on the lowest speed for 1 minute. Cover the bowl and let soak for 1 hour to autolyse (see page 38).

Add the sourdough starter to the dough and mix on medium speed for 1 to 2 minutes. Cover the bowl and let rest for 30 minutes.

Add the salt to the dough and mix on medium speed for 2 to 4 minutes. Cover the bowl and let rest for 30 minutes.

Fun Part
Spray a work surface with water and dump the dough onto it. Wet your hands with water and start stretching the dough and folding it until you feel the tension and strength of it (see page 40). Sprinkle a glass bowl with water to prevent sticking and put the dough into the bowl. Cover the bowl and let rest for 30 minutes.

Perform 3 more coil folds or stretch and folds (see page 42 or 40), each 45 minutes apart. Leave the dough untouched for 30 to 45 minutes until it is puffy and 50 percent bigger than its original size.

Note: If the dough doesn't seem puffy after the third coil fold, let the dough proof for 45 minutes more, then perform one extra coil fold and proceed to the next step.

Preshape the dough (see page 43) and let rest for 30 minutes, uncovered. Then, shape the dough (see page 44).

Transfer the dough to a proofing basket. Cover the dough and let rest for 15 minutes.

Patience
Refrigerate the dough for 8 to 24 hours for the cold fermentation process.

CONTINUED

Next Day

An adult should perform all the actions in these steps while you observe the process. Place a Dutch oven inside the oven and preheat the oven to 500°F (250°C). Let the oven heat for 45 minutes to 1 hour. When the oven is hot, ask an adult to remove the hot pot from the oven. Remove the dough from the refrigerator and flip it onto a piece of parchment paper. Ask an adult helper to score the loaf and transfer it to the Dutch oven. Put the lid on the Dutch oven and bake the dough for 15 minutes. Ask an adult helper to remove the hot lid. Lower the oven temperature to 450°F (230°C) and bake the dough for 25 minutes more until golden brown. An adult should remove the hot pot from the oven and then use the parchment paper to lift the loaf out of the hot Dutch oven and place it on a cooling rack.

Let the loaf cool for 1 to 2 hours before enjoying a slice of freshly baked bread.

Sample Schedule

You will need 5 hours 30 minutes on Day 1 plus an overnight cold fermentation, then 3-plus hours on Day 2 to finish the recipe.

	DAY 1	DAY 2
Mix/soak the water and flours	9:00 a.m.	
Add the starter	10:00 a.m.	
Add the salt	10:30 a.m.	
Stretch/fold	11:00 a.m.	
Coil fold or stretch/fold 1	11:30 a.m.	
Coil fold or stretch/fold 2	12:15 p.m.	
Coil fold or stretch/fold 3	1:00 p.m.	
Preshape	1:45 p.m.	
Shape and proof	2:15 p.m.	
Refrigerate	2:30 p.m.	
Preheat Dutch oven		9:00 a.m.
Bake		9:45 a.m.

BREADCRUMBS

Pain de campagne, which means "country bread" in French, is also called "French sourdough." In centuries past, French villagers brought their dough to communal ovens to be baked. These large, round loafs weighed anywhere from 4 to as much as 12 pounds (1.8 to 5.4 kg) and could feed a family until the next communal baking day.

Butter-Enriched Sourdough Loaf

10 to 12 slices

500 g bread flour

325 g filtered water

100 g active sourdough starter (see page 34)

10 g salt

25 g sugar

25 g butter, at room temperature

See photo on page 48

Who doesn't like to spread some butter on a slice of freshly baked bread? But how about adding some butter into the dough? It's a game changer. The butter makes the loaf so soft and the crust so thin, crunchy, and perfect for lunch sandwiches. You can make the best PB&J on this bread, or spread some butter and jam on it. I promise you'll love it.

Ask an adult to set up a stand mixer fitted with the dough hook attachment. Add the flour and water to the bowl and mix on the lowest speed for 1 minute. Cover the bowl and let soak for 1 hour to autolyse (see page 38).

Add the sourdough starter to the dough and mix on low speed for 1 to 2 minutes. Cover the bowl and let rest for 30 minutes.

Add the salt and sugar. Mix on medium speed for 2 to 3 minutes until well incorporated. Add the room-temperature butter, increase the speed to medium-high, and mix for 3 to 6 minutes until the butter is well incorporated. The dough should be shiny, come together in a ball, but still stick to the bottom of the bowl. Cover the bowl and let rest for 30 minutes.

Fun Part
Spray a work surface with water and dump the dough onto it. Wet your hands with water and start stretching the dough and folding it until you feel the tension and strength of it (see page 40). Sprinkle a glass bowl with water to prevent sticking and put the dough into the bowl. Cover the bowl and let rest for 30 minutes.

Perform 3 more coil folds or stretch and folds (see page 42 or 40), each 45 minutes apart. Leave the dough untouched for 30 to 45 minutes until it is puffy and 50 percent bigger than its original size.

Note: If the dough doesn't seem puffy after the third coil fold, let the dough proof for 45 minutes more, then perform one extra coil fold and proceed to the next step.

Preshape the dough (see page 43) and let rest for 30 minutes, then shape the dough (see page 44). Transfer the dough to a proofing basket. Cover the dough and let rest for 15 minutes.

Patience
Refrigerate the dough for 12 to 24 hours for the cold fermentation process (see page 44).

Next Day

An adult should perform all the actions in these steps while you observe the process. Place a Dutch oven in the oven and preheat the oven to 500°F (250°C). Let the oven heat for 45 minutes to 1 hour. When the oven is hot, ask an adult to remove the pot from the oven. Remove the dough from the refrigerator and flip it onto a piece of parchment paper. Ask a parent or other trusted adult to score the loaf and transfer it to the Dutch oven. Put the lid on the Dutch oven and bake the dough for 15 minutes. Ask an adult helper to remove the hot lid. Lower the oven temperature to 450°F (230°C) and bake the dough for 25 minutes more until golden brown. An adult should remove the hot Dutch oven from the oven and then use the parchment paper to lift the loaf out of the hot Dutch oven and place it on a cooling rack.

Let the loaf cool for 1 to 2 hours before enjoying a slice.

Sample Schedule

You will need 5 hours 30 minutes on Day 1 plus an overnight cold fermentation, then 3-plus hours on Day 2 to finish the recipe.

	DAY 1	DAY 2
Mix/soak the water and flours	9:00 a.m.	
Add the starter	10:00 a.m.	
Add the remaining ingredients	10:30 a.m.	
Stretch/fold	11:00 a.m.	
Coil fold or stretch/fold 1	11:30 a.m.	
Coil fold or stretch/fold 2	12:15 p.m.	
Coil fold or stretch/fold 3	1:00 p.m.	
Preshape	1:45 p.m.	
Shape and proof	2:15 p.m.	
Refrigerate	2:30 p.m.	
Preheat Dutch oven		9:00 a.m.
Bake		9:45 a.m.

Purple Corn Sourdough Loaf

10 to 12 slices

475 g bread flour

25 g plus 60 g purple corn flour

375 g filtered water

100 g active sourdough starter (see page 34)

10 g salt

Purple corn is not only full of nutrients but also full of delicious flavor. Plus, it adds so much brightness to your regular sourdough loaf. My daughter loves everything purple. She is always excited when I bake this bread. Are you excited to try it?

Ask a parent to set up a stand mixer fitted with the dough hook attachment. Add the bread flour, 25 g of the purple corn flour, and water to the bowl and mix on the lowest speed for 1 minute. Cover the bowl and let soak for 1 hour to autolyse (see page 38).

Add the sourdough starter to the bowl and mix on low speed for 1 to 2 minutes. Cover the bowl and let rest for 30 minutes.

Add the salt and mix on medium speed for 2 to 4 minutes. The dough should come together but still stick to the bottom of the bowl. Cover and let rest for 30 minutes.

Fun Part
Spray a work surface with water and dump the dough onto it. Wet your hands with water and start stretching the dough and folding it until you feel the tension and strength of the dough (see page 40). Sprinkle a glass bowl with water to prevent sticking and put the dough in it. Cover the bowl and let rest for 30 minutes.

Perform 3 coil folds or stretches and folds (see page 42 or 40), each 45 minutes apart. Leave the dough untouched for 30 to 45 minutes until it is puffy and 50 percent bigger than its original size.

Note: If the dough doesn't seem puffy after the third coil fold, let the dough proof for 45 minutes more, then perform one extra coil fold and proceed to the next step.

Preshape the dough (see page 43) and let rest for 30 minutes, uncovered, then shape the dough (see page 44).

Place the remaining 60 g of purple corn flour in a large shallow dish. Spray the top of the loaf with water and roll it in the purple corn flour to coat. Transfer the dough to a proofing basket, cover, and let rest for 15 minutes.

Patience
Refrigerate the dough for 12 to 24 hours for the cold fermentation process (see page 44).

CONTINUED

Next Day

An adult should perform all the actions in these steps while you observe the process. Ask as adult to place a Dutch oven inside the oven and preheat the oven to 500°F (250°C). Let the oven heat for 45 minutes to 1 hour. When the oven is hot, ask an adult to remove the pot from the hot oven. Remove the dough from the refrigerator and flip it onto a piece of parchment paper. Ask an adult to score the loaf and transfer it to the Dutch oven. Cover the pot and bake the dough for 15 minutes. Ask an adult to remove the hot lid. Lower the oven temperature to 450°F (230°C) and bake the dough for 25 minutes more until golden brown. An adult should remove the hot pot from the oven and then use the parchment paper to lift the loaf out of the hot Dutch oven and place it on a cooling rack.

Let the loaf cool for 1 to 2 hours before enjoying a slice.

Sample Schedule

You will need 5 hours 30 minutes on Day 1 plus an overnight cold fermentation, then 3-plus hours on Day 2 to finish the recipe.

	DAY 1	DAY 2
Mix/soak the water and flours	9:00 a.m.	
Add the starter	10:00 a.m.	
Add the salt	10:30 a.m.	
Stretch/fold	11:00 a.m.	
Coil fold or stretch/fold 1	11:30 a.m.	
Coil fold or stretch/fold 2	12:15 p.m.	
Coil fold or stretch/fold 3	1:00 p.m.	
Preshape	1:45 p.m.	
Shape, roll in corn flour, and proof	2:15 p.m.	
Refrigerate	2:30 p.m.	
Preheat Dutch oven		9:00 a.m.
Bake		9:45 a.m.

BREADCRUMBS

Purple corn can be traced back to ancient Aztec civilizations. It's still grown in Peru today. The corn is very nutritious; despite its bold color, purple corn is the same species as the yellow corn Americans are most familiar with; however, the more colorful varieties have higher levels of cell-protecting antioxidants.

Potato Sourdough Loaf

10 to 12 slices

250 g mashed boiled white or red potato

500 g bread flour plus 25 g, if needed

250 g filtered water

100 g active sourdough starter (see page 34)

10 g salt

10 g sugar or honey

10 g neutral oil or butter, at room temperature

Adding mashed potato to a loaf of bread sounds weird, right? I never thought that a potato—a simple starchy vegetable—could add so much softness to bread. But then I did some research, and found out that many baked goods contain potato starch or flour, or even actual mashed potato. Potato can be added for special softness and moistness in all kinds of breads, from hamburger and hot dog buns to sweet breads such as brioche or challah. Some bakeries even add the water in which the potatoes were boiled; this simple trick adds so much softness to the dough. Let's try it—you will be surprised by the wonderful taste.

Ask an adult to set up a stand mixer fitted with the dough hook attachment. Add the mashed potato, 500 g of bread flour, and water to the bowl and mix on the lowest speed for 1 minute. Cover the bowl and let soak for 1 hour to autolyse (see page 38).

Add the sourdough starter to the bowl and mix on medium speed for 1 to 2 minutes. Cover the bowl and let rest for 30 minutes.

Add the salt and sugar and mix on low speed for 2 to 3 minutes until well incorporated.

Add the oil and continue mixing for 5 to 10 minutes more. If the dough seems too sticky, add the remaining 25 g of flour. The dough should come together but will still stick to the bottom of the bowl. Cover and let rest for 30 minutes.

Fun Part
Spray the table with water and dump the dough onto it. Wet your hands with water and start stretching the dough and folding it until you feel the tension and strength

of it (see page 40). Sprinkle a glass bowl with water to prevent sticking and put the dough in the bowl. Cover the bowl and let rest for 30 min.

Perform 3 coil folds or stretches and folds (see page 42 or 40), each 45 minutes apart. Leave the dough untouched for 30 to 45 minutes until it is puffy and 50 percent bigger than its original size.

Note: If the dough doesn't seem puffy after the third coil fold, let the dough proof for 45 minutes more, then perform one extra coil fold and proceed to the next step.

Preshape the dough (see page 43) and let rest for 30 minutes, then shape the dough (see page 44). Transfer the dough to a proofing basket, cover, and let rest for 15 minutes.

Patience
Refrigerate the dough for 12 to 24 hours for the cold fermentation process (see page 44).

CONTINUED

Next Day

An adult should perform all the actions in these steps while you observe the process. Ask an adult to place a Dutch oven inside the oven and preheat the oven to 500°F (250°C). Let the oven heat for 45 minutes to 1 hour. When the oven is hot, ask an adult to remove the pot from the oven. Remove the dough from the refrigerator and flip it onto a piece of parchment paper. Ask an adult to score the loaf and transfer it to the Dutch oven. Cover the pot and bake the dough for 15 minutes. Ask a parent or other trusted adult to remove the hot lid. Lower the oven temperature to 450°F (230°C) and bake the dough for 25 minutes more until golden brown. An adult should remove the hot Dutch oven from the oven and then use the parchment paper to lift the loaf out of the hot Dutch oven and place it on a cooling rack.

Let the loaf cool for 1 to 2 hours before enjoying a slice.

Sample Schedule

You will need 5 hours 30 minutes on Day 1 plus an overnight cold fermentation, then 3-plus hours on Day 2 to finish the recipe.

	DAY 1	DAY 2
Mix/soak the potato, water, and flour	9:00 a.m.	
Add the starter	10:00 a.m.	
Add the remaining ingredients	10:30 a.m.	
Stretch/fold	11:00 a.m.	
Coil fold or stretch/fold 1	11:30 a.m.	
Coil fold or stretch/fold 2	12:15 p.m.	
Coil fold or stretch/fold 3	1:00 p.m.	
Preshape	1:45 p.m.	
Shape and proof	2:15 p.m.	
Refrigerate	2:30 p.m.	
Preheat Dutch oven		9:00 a.m.
Bake		9:45 a.m.

BREADCRUMBS

In 1995, potatoes became the first vegetable grown in space, both to feed the astronauts on their missions and, eventually, to feed future space colonies.

Jalapeño-Cheddar Sourdough Loaf

10 to 12 slices

If you don't have time to prepare a midday meal, this loaf is great to have for lunch or dinner. It's a complete meal in one slice, melty Cheddar cheese plus spicy jalapeño peppers. The bread also can be paired with your favorite soup or salad. It's a winning combination—trust me.

DOUGH

450 g bread flour

50 g whole wheat, whole grain flour

385 g filtered water

100 g active sourdough starter (see page 34)

10 g salt

FILLING

½ cup (68 g) sliced pickled jalapeño peppers

⅔ cup (80 g) cubed Cheddar cheese

To make the dough: Ask an adult to set up a stand mixer fitted with the dough hook attachment. Add the flours and water to the bowl and mix on the lowest speed for 1 minute. Cover the bowl and let soak for 1 hour to autolyse (see page 38).

Add the sourdough starter to the bowl and mix on low speed for 1 to 2 minutes. Cover the bowl and let rest for 30 minutes.

Add the salt and mix on medium speed for 2 to 3 minutes until well incorporated. The dough should come together but will still stick to the bottom of the bowl. Cover and let rest for 30 minutes.

To fill the dough: Pat the jalapeño slices dry with paper towels to remove excess liquid.

Fun Part

Spray a work surface with water and dump the dough onto it. Wet your hands with water and stretch the dough using the lamination process (see page 40). Sprinkle the jalapeño slices and cheese cubes over the dough, then fold the ingredients into the dough. Spray a glass dish with water to prevent sticking and transfer the dough to it. Cover the bowl and let rest for 30 minutes.

Perform 3 stretches and folds (see page 40), each 45 minutes apart. Leave the dough untouched for 30 to 45 minutes until it is puffy and 50 percent bigger than its original size.

Note: If the dough doesn't seem puffy after the third fold, let the dough proof for 45 minutes more, then perform one extra fold and proceed to the next step.

Preshape the dough (see page 43) and let it rest for 30 minutes, then shape the dough (see page 40). Transfer the dough to a proofing basket, cover, and let rest for 15 minutes.

Patience

Refrigerate the dough for 12 to 24 hours for the cold fermentation process (see page 44).

CONTINUED

Next Day

An adult should perform all the actions in these steps while you observe the process. Ask an adult to place a Dutch oven inside the oven and preheat the oven to 500°F (250°C). Let the oven heat for 45 minutes to 1 hour. When the oven is hot, ask an adult to remove the pot from the oven. Remove the dough from the refrigerator and flip it onto a piece of parchment paper. Ask an adult to score the loaf and transfer it to the Dutch oven. Cover the pot and bake the dough for 15 minutes. Ask an adult to remove the hot lid. Lower the oven temperature to 450°F (230°C) and bake the dough for 25 minutes more until golden brown. An adult should remove the hot pot from the oven and then use the parchment paper to lift the loaf out of the hot Dutch oven and place it on a cooling rack.

Let the loaf cool for 1 to 2 hours before enjoying a slice.

BREADCRUMBS

After you strain the jalapeño slices, you should pat them dry with a paper towel so you don't add too much extra liquid to the dough.

Sample Schedule

You will need 6 hours on Day 1 plus an overnight cold fermentation, then 3-plus hours on Day 2 to finish the recipe.

	DAY 1	DAY 2
Mix/soak the water and flours	9:00 a.m.	
Add the starter	10:00 a.m.	
Add the salt	10:30 a.m.	
Stretch/fold	11:00 a.m.	
Add jalapeño and cheese	11:30 a.m.	
Stretch/fold 1	12:00 p.m.	
Stretch/fold 2	12:45 p.m.	
Stretch/fold 3	1:30 p.m.	
Preshape	2:15 p.m.	
Shape and proof	2:45 p.m.	
Refrigerate	3:00 p.m.	
Preheat Dutch oven		9:00 a.m.
Bake		9:45 a.m.

The Softest Milk Sandwich Loaf

10 to 12 slices

TANGZHONG
200 g filtered water

100 g bread flour

DOUGH
265 g lukewarm
(100°F or 38°C) milk

0.5 to 1 g active dry yeast
(optional)

50 g sugar

100 g active sourdough
starter (see page 34)

300 g tangzhong
(the complete amount
you made)

500 g bread flour,
plus more for dusting

10 g salt

50 g butter, at room
temperature

This recipe is also known as Hokkaido milk bread, using an Asian breadmaking technique called the tangzhong method. I first tried Hokkaido milk bread at a Japanese market. It is very light and fluffy and chewy, all at the same time, with a light hint of sweetness. In this recipe, instead of commercial yeast, I use sourdough starter and it comes out delicious. Adding sourdough starter to the bread helps it stay fresher and softer longer.

The tangzhong method helps you achieve a soft bread texture. Also called a water roux, when some amount of flour cooks in hot boiling water, the method causes the dough's starch to gelatinize. Since dough for milk bread includes enrichments (such as sugar and butter), it might extend the proofing time.

Also, using sourdough starter in enriched dough may produce a tangy flavor in the final product. Bakers use a small trick to reduce the sourness of the final product; they add a tiny amount of commercial yeast to the dough, which speeds up the fermentation process and reduces the acidity of the finished bread. With or without yeast, milk bread is delicious.

To make the tangzhong: The tangzhong has to be prepared at least 1 hour ahead of making the bread dough, or the night before. Ask an adult to help you with this step. In a small saucepan, bring the water to a boil. Reduce the heat to low and stir in the flour. Cook for 1 to 2 minutes, stirring, until you get a thick paste. Remove from the heat and let cool. Cover and refrigerate until needed.

Next Day
To make the dough: Ask an adult to set up a stand mixer fitted with the dough hook attachment. In the bowl of the stand mixer, stir together the lukewarm milk and yeast (if using). Stir in the sugar, sourdough starter, tangzhong, and flour. Cover the bowl and let soak for 1 hour to autolyse (see page 38).

Mix the dough on medium speed for 3 to 4 minutes until well incorporated.

Add the salt and mix for 2 minutes more. The dough should come together.

Add the butter and mix for 10 to 15 minutes until well incorporated and the dough comes together and looks shiny.

Perform a windowpane test (see page 38).

CONTINUED

Sample Schedule

After making the tangzhong the evening before baking this bread, you will need about 7 hours to finish this recipe.

	DAY 1	DAY 2
Make the tangzhong	Evening	
Mix/soak the milk, sugar, starter, tangzhong, and flour		9:00 a.m.
Mix dough and add the salt and butter		10:00 a.m.
Cover and proof (with 2 stretch/folds)		10:15 a.m.
Shape and proof		2:15 p.m.
Bake		6:15 p.m.

Cover the dough and let it proof for 3 to 4 hours at a temperature between 76°F and 80°F (24.5°C and 27°C). During the proofing time, perform 2 stretches and folds (see page 40). The dough should become slightly puffy.

Fun Part

Dust a work surface with flour and dump the dough onto it. Stretch the dough into a rectangular shape, about 13 × 4 inches (33 × 10 cm), to match the size of your loaf pan. Roll the dough rectangle into a tight roll (see page 45).

Line a baking pan with parchment paper. Transfer the roll to the prepared baking pan.

Patience

Cover the dough and let it proof for 4 to 6 hours in a warm place, at a temperature between 76°F and 80°F (24.5°C and 27°C), until it doubles, or more, in volume.

Note: If it's too cold in your house, use your oven with the light on as a proofing chamber. If you didn't add yeast to the dough, the final proof might take longer. When the bread is proofed, sprinkle some flour on top.

Ask an adult to preheat the oven to 375°F (190°C).

Ask a parent or other trusted adult to place the baking pan into the oven. Bake the dough for 35 to 40 minutes until golden brown. Ask an adult to remove the hot loaf from the oven and then use the parchment paper to lift the loaf out of the hot pan and place it on a cooling rack.

Let it cool for 1 hour and enjoy.

Double Chocolate Sourdough Loaf

10 to 12 slices

Who doesn't like chocolate? How about a double chocolate loaf of sourdough bread that you can make yourself? It is both intriguing and delicious. When you bake this loaf, your house will smell like a chocolate factory and your family will be asking how soon it will be ready to eat.

DOUGH
450 g bread flour

50 g whole wheat, whole grain flour

375 g filtered water

100 g active sourdough starter (see page 34)

10 g salt

25 g sugar

FILLING
Scant ⅓ cup (32 g) cocoa powder

½ cup plus 1 tablespoon (100 g) dark chocolate chips

To make the dough: Ask an adult to set up a stand mixer fitted with the dough hook attachment. Add the flour and water to the bowl and mix on the lowest speed for 1 minute. Cover the bowl and let soak for 1 hour to autolyse (see page 38).

Add the sourdough starter to the bowl and mix on medium speed for 1 to 2 minutes. Cover the bowl and let rest for 30 minutes.

Add the salt and sugar and mix on medium speed for 2 to 4 minutes until well incorporated. The dough should come together, but will still stick to the bottom of the bowl. Cover and let rest for 30 minutes.

Fun Part
To fill the dough: Spray a work surface with water and dump the dough onto it. Wet your hands with water and stretch the dough using the lamination process (see page 40). Sprinkle the cocoa powder all over the dough's surface. Spritz some water on the cocoa powder. Cocoa tends to steal hydration away from the dough, so the water will return the hydration to the dough. Then, scatter the chocolate chips all over the dough. Fold the dough and it let rest for 45 minutes.

Spray a glass dish with water to prevent sticking and transfer the dough to it. Cover the bowl and let rest for 30 minutes.

Perform 3 coil folds or stretches and folds (see page 42 or 40), each 45 minutes apart. Leave the dough untouched for 30 to 45 minutes until it is puffy and 50 percent bigger than its original size.

Note: If the dough doesn't seem puffy after the third coil fold, let the dough proof for 45 minutes more, then perform one extra coil fold and proceed to the next step.

Preshape the dough (see page 43) and let it rest for 30 minutes, then shape the dough (see page 44). Transfer the dough to a proofing basket, cover, and let rest for 15 minutes.

Patience
Refrigerate the dough for 12 to 24 hours for the cold fermentation process (see page 44).

CONTINUED

Next Day

An adult should perform all the actions in these steps while you observe the process. Ask an adult to place a Dutch oven inside the oven and preheat the oven to 500°F (250°C). Let the oven heat for 45 minutes to 1 hour. When the oven is hot, ask an adult to remove the pot from the oven. Remove the dough from the refrigerator and flip it onto a piece of parchment paper. Ask an adult to score the loaf and transfer it to the Dutch oven. Cover the pot and bake the dough for 15 minutes. Ask an adult to remove the hot lid. Lower the oven temperature to 450°F (230°C) and bake the dough for 25 minutes more until golden brown. An adult should remove the hot pot from the oven and then use the parchment paper to lift the loaf out of the hot Dutch oven and place it on a cooling rack.

Let the loaf cool for 1 to 2 hours before enjoying a slice.

BREADCRUMBS

Dark chocolate can be enjoyed as a part of a balanced heart-healthy diet and lifestyle. But did you know that it takes 400 cocoa beans to make 1 pound (454 g) of chocolate and each cacao tree produces about 2,500 beans? That's a lot of trees for some chocolate!

Sample Schedule

You will need 6 hours 15 minutes on Day 1 plus an overnight cold fermentation, then 3-plus hours on Day 2 to finish the recipe.

	DAY 1	DAY 2
Mix/soak the water and flour	9:00 a.m.	
Add the starter	10:00 a.m.	
Add the salt and sugar	10:30 a.m.	
Stretch/fold and add cocoa and chocolate chips	11:00 a.m.	
Transfer dough	11:45 a.m.	
Coil fold or stretch/fold 1	12:15 p.m.	
Coil fold or stretch/fold 2	1:00 p.m.	
Coil fold or stretch/fold 3	1:45 p.m.	
Preshape	2:30 p.m.	
Shape and proof	3:00 p.m.	
Refrigerate	3:15 p.m.	
Preheat Dutch oven		9:00 a.m.
Bake		9:45 a.m.

Cinnamon-Raisin Sourdough Loaf

10 to 12 slices

The cinnamon and raisin combination will bring some warmth and comfort to your home during colder and gloomy days. A slice of this bread spread with butter or cream cheese makes a delicious breakfast.

DOUGH

450 g bread flour

50 g whole wheat, whole grain flour

390 g filtered water

100 g active sourdough starter (see page 34)

10 g salt

25 g sugar

FILLING

1 tablespoon plus 1 teaspoon (12 g) ground cinnamon

⅔ cup (100 g) raisins, washed and dried

To make the dough: Ask an adult to set up a stand mixer fitted with the dough hook attachment. Add the flours and water to the bowl and mix on the lowest speed for 1 minute. Cover the bowl and let soak for 1 hour to autolyse (see page 38).

Add the sourdough starter to the bowl and mix on medium speed for 1 to 2 minutes. Cover the bowl and let rest for 30 minutes.

Add the salt and sugar and mix on medium speed for 2 to 4 minutes until well incorporated. The dough should come together, but will still stick to the bottom of the bowl. Cover and let rest for 30 minutes.

Fun Part

To fill the dough: Spray a work surface with water and dump the dough onto it. Wet your hands with water and stretch the dough using the lamination process (see page 40). Sprinkle the cinnamon and raisins all over the dough, then fold the ingredients into the dough. Spray a glass dish with water to prevent sticking and transfer the dough to it. Cover and let rest for 30 minutes.

Perform 3 stretches and folds (see page 40), each 45 minutes apart. Leave the dough untouched for 30 to 45 minutes until it is puffy and 50 percent bigger than its original size.

Note: If the dough doesn't seem puffy after the third fold, let the dough proof for 45 minutes more, then perform one extra fold and proceed to the next step.

Preshape the dough (see page 43) and let it rest for 30 minutes, then shape the dough (see page 44). Transfer the dough to a proofing basket, cover, and let rest for 15 minutes.

Patience

Refrigerate the dough for 12 to 24 hours for the cold fermentation process (see page 44).

Next Day

An adult should perform all the actions in these steps while you observe the process. Ask an adult to place a Dutch oven inside the oven and preheat the oven to 500°F (250°C). Let the oven heat for 45 minutes to 1 hour.

CONTINUED

Once the oven is hot, ask an adult to remove the pot from the oven. Remove the dough from the refrigerator and flip it onto a piece of parchment paper. Ask an adult to score the loaf and transfer it to the Dutch oven. Cover the pot and bake the dough for 15 minutes. Ask an adult to remove the hot lid. Lower the oven temperature to 450°F (230°C) and bake the dough for 25 minutes more until golden brown. An adult should remove the hot pot from the oven and then use the parchment paper to lift the loaf out of the hot Dutch oven and place it on a cooling rack.

Let the loaf cool for 1 to 2 hours before enjoying a slice.

BREADCRUMBS

Cinnamon-raison bread also makes delicious French toast and bread pudding. You can find lots of recipes online!

Sample Schedule

You will need 5 hours 30 minutes on Day 1 plus an overnight cold fermentation, then 3-plus hours on Day 2 to finish the recipe.

	DAY 1	DAY 2
Mix/soak the water and flour	9:00 a.m.	
Add the starter	10:00 a.m.	
Add the salt and sugar	10:30 a.m.	
Stretch/fold and add the cinnamon and raisins	11:00 a.m.	
Stretch/fold 1	11:30 a.m.	
Stretch/fold 2	12:15 p.m.	
Stretch/fold 3	1:00 p.m.	
Preshape	1:45 p.m.	
Shape and proof	2:15 p.m.	
Refrigerate	2:30 p.m.	
Preheat Dutch oven		9:00 a.m.
Bake		9:45 a.m.

Turmeric and Poppy Seed Sourdough Loaf

10 to 12 slices

450 g bread flour

50 g whole wheat, whole grain flour

10 g ground turmeric

385 g filtered water

100 g active sourdough starter (see page 34)

10 g salt

40 g poppy seeds

Every time I bake this bread, it brings so much sunshine and brightness to our kitchen table. Turmeric makes the bread so colorful and poppy seeds give more structure and flavor to the loaf. My family loves it. I hope you will, too.

Ask an adult to set up a stand mixer fitted with the dough hook attachment. Add the flours, turmeric, and water to the bowl and mix on the lowest speed for 1 minute. Cover the bowl and let soak for 1 hour to autolyse (see page 38).

Add the sourdough starter to the bowl and mix on medium speed for 1 to 2 minutes. Cover the bowl and let rest for 30 minutes.

Add the salt and mix on low speed for 2 to 4 minutes until well incorporated. The dough should come together, but will still stick to the bottom of the bowl. Cover and let rest for 30 minutes.

Fun Part
Spray a work surface with water and dump the dough onto it. Wet your hands with water and stretch the dough using the lamination process (see page 40). Sprinkle the poppy seeds over the dough, then fold them into the dough. Spray a glass dish with water to prevent sticking and transfer the dough to it. Cover and let rest for 30 minutes.

Perform 3 coil folds or stretches and folds (see page 42 or 40), each 45 minutes apart. Leave the dough untouched for 30 to 45 minutes until it is puffy and 50 percent bigger than its original size.

Note: If the dough doesn't seem puffy after the third coil fold, let the dough proof for 45 minutes more, then perform one extra coil fold and proceed to the next step.

Preshape the dough (see page 43) and let it rest for 30 minutes, then shape the dough (see page 40). Transfer the dough to a proofing basket, cover and let rest for 15 minutes.

Patience
Refrigerate the dough for 12 to 24 hours for the cold fermentation process (see page 44).

CONTINUED

Next Day

An adult should perform all the actions in these steps while you observe the process. Ask an adult to place a Dutch oven inside the oven and preheat the oven to 500°F (250°C). Let the oven heat for 45 minutes to 1 hour. When the oven is hot, ask an adult to remove the pot. Remove the dough from the refrigerator and flip it onto a piece of parchment paper. Ask an adult to score the loaf and transfer it to the Dutch oven. Cover the pot and bake the dough for 15 minutes. Ask an adult to remove the hot lid. Lower the oven temperature to 450°F (230°C) and bake the dough for 25 minutes more until golden brown. An adult should remove the hot pot from the oven and then use the parchment paper to lift the loaf out of the hot Dutch oven and place it on a cooling rack.

Let the loaf cool for 1 to 2 hours before enjoying a slice.

Sample Schedule

You will need 5 hours 30 minutes on Day 1 plus an overnight cold fermentation, then 3-plus hours on Day 2 to finish the recipe.

	DAY 1	DAY 2
Mix/soak the water, turmeric, and flour	9:00 a.m.	
Add the starter	10:00 a.m.	
Add the salt	10:30 a.m.	
Stretch/fold and add the poppy seeds	11:00 a.m.	
Coil fold or stretch/fold 1	11:30 a.m.	
Coil fold or stretch/fold 2	12:15 p.m.	
Coil fold or stretch/fold 3	1:00 p.m.	
Preshape	1:45 p.m.	
Shape and proof	2:15 p.m.	
Refrigerate	2:30 p.m.	
Preheat Dutch oven		9:00 a.m.
Bake		9:45 a.m.

Sweet S'mores Sourdough Loaf

10 to 12 slices

No matter the season, one word will always remind me of crackling summertime fires and happy kids creating the sweetest dessert of all time: s'mores. When it's cold and snowy, my kids jump around the kitchen, waiting for one of their favorite treats—a sourdough loaf filled with marshmallows and milk chocolate and covered with a crispy graham cracker coating.

To make the dough: Ask an adult to set up a stand mixer fitted with the dough hook attachment. Add the flours and water to the bowl and mix on the lowest speed for 1 minute. Cover the bowl and let soak for 1 hour to autolyse (see page 38).

Add the sourdough starter to the bowl and mix on medium speed for 1 to 2 minutes. Cover the bowl and let rest for 30 minutes.

Add the salt and sugar and mix on medium speed for 2 to 4 minutes until well incorporated. The dough should come together, but still stick to the bottom of the bowl. Cover and let rest for 30 minutes.

Fun Part
To fill the dough: Spray a work surface with water and dump the dough onto it. Wet your hands with water and stretch the dough using the lamination process (see page 40). Scatter the chocolate chips and marshmallows all over the dough, then fold the ingredients into the dough. Spray a glass baking dish with water to prevent sticking and transfer the dough to it. Cover and let rest for 30 minutes.

Perform 3 coil folds or stretches and folds (see page 42 or 40), each 45 minutes apart. Leave the dough untouched for 30 to 45 minutes until it is puffy and 50 percent bigger than its original size.

Note: If the dough doesn't seem puffy after the third coil fold, let the dough proof for 45 minutes more, then perform one extra coil fold and proceed to the next step.

Preshape the dough (see page 43) and let it rest for 30 minutes, then shape the dough (see page 44).

To coat the dough: Place the graham cracker crumbs in a large shallow bowl. Spray the top of the loaf with water and roll it in the crumbs. Transfer the dough to a proofing basket, cover, and let rest for 15 minutes.

Patience
Refrigerate the dough for 12 to 24 hours for the cold fermentation process (see page 44).

CONTINUED

DOUGH
450 g bread flour

50 g whole wheat, whole grain flour

390 g filtered water

100 g active sourdough starter (see page 34)

10 g salt

25 g sugar

S'MORES FILLING
Heaping ⅓ to scant ⅔ cup (58 to 117 g) milk chocolate chips

1½ cups (75 g) mini marshmallows, plus more as needed (see Note, page 80)

COATING
1 cup (84 g) crushed graham crackers

Next Day

An adult should perform all the actions in these steps while you observe the process. Ask an adult to place a Dutch oven inside the oven and preheat the oven to 500°F (250°C). Let the oven heat for 45 minutes to 1 hour. When the oven is hot, ask an adult to remove the pot from the oven. Remove the dough from the refrigerator and flip it onto a piece of parchment paper. Ask an adult to score the loaf and transfer it to the Dutch oven. Cover the pot and bake the dough for 15 minutes. Ask an adult to remove the hot lid. Lower the oven temperature to 450°F (230°C) and bake for 20 minutes more until golden brown.

Note: Most likely, the marshmallows will melt inside the loaf during baking; if you would like more marshmallows, ask an adult to sprinkle more on top of the loaf 2 to 3 minutes before the end of the baking time.

An adult should remove the hot pot from the oven and then use the parchment paper to lift the loaf out of the hot Dutch oven and place it on a cooling rack.

Let the loaf cool for 1 to 2 hours before enjoying a slice.

Sample Schedule

You will need 5 hours 30 minutes on Day 1 plus an overnight cold fermentation, then 3-plus hours on Day 2 to finish the recipe.

	DAY 1	DAY 2
Mix/soak the water and flour	9:00 a.m.	
Add the starter	10:00 a.m.	
Add the salt and sugar	10:30 a.m.	
Stretch/fold and add the chocolate chips and marshmallows	11:00 a.m.	
Coil fold or stretch/fold 1	11:30 a.m.	
Coil fold or stretch/fold 2	12:15 p.m.	
Coil fold or stretch/fold 3	1:00 p.m.	
Preshape	1:45 p.m.	
Shape, roll in graham crackers, and proof	2:15 p.m.	
Refrigerate	2:30 p.m.	
Preheat Dutch oven		9:00 a.m.
Bake		9:45 a.m.

BREADCRUMBS

The first record of s'mores was found in the Girl Scouts handbook in 1927. Do you think they ever imagined you'd be turning their special campfire treat into yummy bread?

Sourdough Pizza Dough

2 medium-size pizzas, about 10 ounces (290 g) each

300 g bread flour

219 g filtered water

60 g active sourdough starter (see page 34)

6 g salt

6 g olive oil, plus more for coating

Semolina flour, for shaping the pizza

Toppings of choice

This is the best pizza dough recipe I've tried so far; it works perfectly for the home oven. It can be baked on a pizza stone or on a regular baking sheet. My family and I enjoy the process of making pizza on the weekends. Everyone chooses different toppings and then we share it all. For this recipe, start making the dough a day ahead.

Ask an adult to set up a stand mixer fitted with the dough hook attachment. Add the bread flour and water to the bowl and mix on the lowest speed for 1 minute. Cover the bowl and let soak for 1 hour to autolyse (see page 38).

Add the sourdough starter to the bowl and mix on medium speed for 1 to 2 minutes. Cover the bowl and let rest for 30 minutes.

Add the salt and mix on medium speed for 3 to 5 minutes until well incorporated. Add the olive oil and continue mixing until the dough comes together but still sticks to the bottom of the bowl. Cover and let rest for 30 minutes.

Fun Part
Spray a work surface with water and dump the dough onto it. Wet your hands with water and stretch and fold the dough until you feel the tension and strength of it (see page 40).

Coat a large bowl with olive oil and transfer the dough to it. Cover the bowl and let rest for 30 minutes.

Perform 3 coil folds or stretches and folds (see page 42 or 40), each 45 minutes apart.

Leave the dough untouched for 30 to 45 minutes until it is big and puffy.

Note: If the dough didn't rise enough, let it sit for 45 minutes and perform one extra stretch and fold. If the dough seems overproofed, shorten the time between stretches and folds to 30 minutes.

Patience
Fold the dough one last time, cover it, and refrigerate for 12 to 24 hours for cold fermentation (see page 44).

Remove the dough from the refrigerator and dump it onto a nonfloured surface. Divide it into 2 equal pieces. Round each piece by pinching all the sides up and flip it onto the opposite side (the smooth surface should be on top; see page 44). Let the dough balls rest, uncovered, for 30 minutes.

Generously sprinkle a baking sheet with semolina flour. Round the pizza dough balls again and transfer them to the prepared baking sheet. Cover the dough with plastic wrap.

CONTINUED

Patience

Let the dough proof for 1 hour 30 minutes, at a temperature between 74°F and 78°F (23°C and 26°C).

While the dough proofs, ask an adult to place a baking stone or baking sheet inside the oven and preheat the oven to 500°F (250°C). Let the oven heat for 1 hour. Prepare your toppings of choice.

Fun Part

It's time to shape your pizza! Dust a work surface with flour and place the dough ball on it. Put some flour on your hands and use them to press the dough down into a flat circle.

With your palms, press the dough down further so it spreads out from the center. Move your hand around the entire circle, pressing down with your palm, so the dough continues to flatten and spread out.

Use your other hand to rotate the dough and stretch it out further as you press. This will help flatten the dough without popping the air bubbles inside. Continue stretching and flattening until your dough is the size and thickness you want.

Sprinkle a piece of parchment paper with a generous amount of semolina flour. Transfer the shaped dough onto the parchment and add your toppings. Ask a parent or other trusted adult to help you transfer the pizza on the parchment onto the baking stone or baking sheet in the very hot oven. Bake for 10 to 15 minutes until the crust is golden brown.

Sample Schedule

You will need 4 hours 45 minutes on Day 1, then 2 hours on Day 2 to finish your pizza, plus about 15 minutes to bake.

	DAY 1	DAY 2
Mix/soak the water and flour	9:00 a.m.	
Add the starter	10:00 a.m.	
Add the salt and oil	10:30 a.m.	
Stretch/fold dough and place in an oiled bowl	11:00 a.m.	
Coil fold or stretch/fold 1	11:30 a.m.	
Coil fold or stretch/fold 2	12:15 p.m.	
Coil fold or stretch/fold 3	1:00 p.m.	
Fold dough and refrigerate	1:45 p.m.	
Round and rest		10:00 a.m.
Round and proof		10:30 a.m.
Preheat oven		11:00 a.m.
Roll out the dough, add toppings, and bake		12:00 p.m.

BREADCRUMBS

According to the website *Slice*, 350 slices of pizza are eaten each second in the United States. I wonder what that number is in Italy . . . ?

Sourdough Challah

1 challah loaf

SOURDOUGH STARTER
Ripe (seed) starter:
1 tablespoon | 15 grams

Filtered water:
¼ cup | 60 grams

Bread flour:
6 tablespoons | 45 grams

Whole wheat,
whole grain flour:
2 tablespoons | 15 grams

DOUGH
110 g active sourdough
starter (see page 34)

80 g sugar

12 g salt, plus more
for the egg wash

210 g lukewarm (100°F or
38°C) filtered water

1 g active dry yeast
(optional)

560 g bread flour

2 large eggs

60 g neutral oil, plus more
for the work surface

Challah was my grandmother's favorite bread. She always made us challah sandwiches with butter and jam. Every year on her birthday, I make a couple of loaves to bring back memories. Using sourdough starter in the dough makes it stay fresh longer. That's what I like most.

Since challah dough includes enrichments, such as sugar, oil, and eggs, it might extend the proofing time. Also, when we use sourdough starter in enriched doughs like challah, the final product may have a tangy flavor. Bakers use a small trick to reduce the sourness of the final product: They add a tiny amount of commercial yeast to the dough, which also speeds up the fermentation process. With or without yeast, challah is delicious.

To make the sourdough starter: In a jar, stir together the starter, water, bread flour, and whole wheat, whole grain flour. Loosely cover the jar and let the starter ferment at room temperature for 4 to 6 hours until it reaches its peak, or overnight until it doubles, or more, in volume.

Next Day
To make the dough: The next day, when the starter is ready, ask an adult to set up a stand mixer fitted with the dough hook attachment. In the mixer's bowl, dissolve the sourdough starter, sugar, and salt in the lukewarm water. Add the yeast (if using) and mix to combine.

Measure 3 tablespoons (22.5 g) of bread flour and set aside. Add the remaining flour and one egg to the bowl. Mix on low speed for 3 to 5 minute until the dough comes together.

Slowly pour in the oil and mix for 15 minutes until the ingredients are well incorporated and the dough comes together.

Note: If the dough is too sticky, gradually mix in the reserved flour. Let the dough mix, then add more flour, if needed. If the dough is too stiff, add some water.

Fun Part
Perform a windowpane test (see page 38).

Round the dough, cover it with plastic wrap, and let it proof for 3 to 4 hours at a temperature between 76°F and 80°F (24.5°C and 27°C).

Note: If it's too cold in your house, use your oven with the light on as a proofing chamber.

CONTINUED

Start with three thin ropes of dough.

Sample Schedule

After making the starter the evening before baking the challah, you will need about 9 hours 15 minutes on Day 2 to finish the recipe.

	DAY 1	DAY 2
Make the challah starter	Evening	
Combine ingredients		9:00 a.m.
Round dough and proof (including 2 stretch/folds)		10:00 a.m.
Preshape		2:00 p.m.
Braid dough and proof		2:15 p.m.
Egg wash and bake		5:15 p.m.

Braid the ropes together.

Roll the ends under.

During the proofing time, perform 2 stretches and folds (see page 40). The dough should become slightly puffy.

Lightly oil a work surface and dump the dough onto it. Ask an adult to use a scraper or bench knife to divide the dough into 3 equal pieces. Preshape each piece of the dough into a cylinder. Cover and let rest for 15 minutes.

Roll each cylinder into a long rope, 15 to 20 inches long (38 to 50 cm).

Fun Part

Now, you can braid the ropes into a three-braid challah. Ask an adult to guide you with the braiding (see page 86).

Line a baking sheet with parchment paper and transfer the braided challah onto the prepared baking sheet.

Patience

Cover the challah and let it proof for 2 to 4 hours at a temperature between 76°F and 80°F (24.5°C and 27°C) until it doubles in volume.

Note: If it's too cold in your house, use your oven with the light on as a proofing chamber.

Ask an adult to preheat the oven to 375°F (190°C).

Prepare an egg wash: In a small bowl, whisk the remaining egg with a little water and a pinch of salt until blended. Using a pastry brush, spread the egg wash all over the challah.

Ask a parent or other trusted adult to place the baking sheet into the oven. Bake the challah for 30 to 40 minutes until golden brown. Ask an adult to help you to remove the hot challah from the oven. Let it cool for at least 1 hour and enjoy.

✦ Tips

Use water from cooking potatoes (instead of a regular water) to add extra softness to your challah. Add raisins or chocolate chips during the final mix to make it more delicious.

Sourdough Cinnamon Buns

6 large buns

SOURDOUGH STARTER
Ripe (seed) starter
(see page 34):
2 tablespoons plus
2 teaspoons | 40 grams

Filtered water:
5 tablespoons plus
1 teaspoon | 80 grams

Bread flour:
9 tablespoons plus
1 teaspoon | 70 grams

Whole wheat, whole
grain flour:
scant 1½ teaspoons |
10 grams

DOUGH
150 g ripe (seed)
sourdough starter

130 g lukewarm (100°F
or 38°C) milk

1 large egg

1 large egg yolk

300 g unbleached
all-purpose flour or bread
flour, plus more as needed

1 g active dry yeast
(optional)

45 g granulated sugar

5 g salt

4 tablespoons (½ stick;
56 g) butter, at room
temperature

CINNAMON FILLING
Scant ½ cup (100 g) light
brown sugar

2 scant tablespoons
(15 g) unbleached
all-purpose flour

1 tablespoon (8 g) ground
cinnamon

Pinch of salt

1 tablespoon plus
1 teaspoon (19 g)
butter, melted

CREAM CHEESE ICING
3 tablespoons (50 g)
cream cheese, at room
temperature

4 tablespoons (½ stick) plus
2 teaspoons (66 g) butter,
at room temperature

2 tablespoons (30 g) milk

1 teaspoon (4.3 g) vanilla
extract

1¼ cups (150 g)
powdered sugar

These delicious cinnamon buns are a family favorite. The dough for cinnamon buns includes enrichments, such as sugar, oil, and eggs, which might extend the proofing time. Also, when we use sourdough starter in enriched dough, the final product could have a tangy flavor. If you'd like to reduce the sourness, add some yeast like you did with the challah bread (page 85).

To make the sourdough starter: In a jar, stir together the starter, water, bread flour, and whole wheat, whole grain flour. Loosely cover the jar and let the starter ferment at room temperature for 4 to 6 hours or overnight until it doubles or more in volume.

To make the dough: In the bowl of a stand mixer, stir together the starter, lukewarm milk, egg, egg yolk, flour, yeast (if using), and granulated sugar. Cover the bowl and let soak for 1 hour to autolyse (see page 38).

After the autolyse, ask an adult to set up a stand mixer fitted with the dough hook attachment. Add the salt to the dough and mix for about 2 minutes on low speed until fully incorporated. Increase the speed to medium and add the butter. Mix the dough for 10 to 15 minutes until it comes together. The dough should become nice and smooth with a shiny appearance.

Note: If the dough seems too sticky, add a little more flour (2 to 3 tablespoons, about 20 g), but don't add a lot of flour because the dough should remain a little sticky. With stretches and folds, it will get stronger and less sticky.

CONTINUED

STICKY BUNS

4 tablespoons (½ stick, or 60 g) butter, at room temperature

Scant ½ cup (100 g) light brown sugar

½ cup (50 g) chopped pecans (optional)

After forming your dough rectangle, spread the butter all over the dough. Sprinkle it with the brown sugar and pecans, and roll the dough into a log. Finish the recipe as directed.

* * *

EUROPEAN POPPY SEED BUNS

1 cup (145 g) poppy seeds

1 cup (200 g) sugar, plus 2 tablespoons (25 g)

1 cup (240 g) milk

1 large egg white

Start working on the filling first: Rinse the poppy seeds, put them in a small saucepan over low heat, and add 1 cup (200 g) of the sugar and the milk. Bring to a boil and cook for about 30 minutes.

Remove the pan from the heat, cover it with a lid, and let sit for 1 to 2 hours to soak and soften.

Before using, strain the poppy seeds and put them in a food processor. Process until you see the seeds breaking apart and you can see their white centers. Add the egg white and remaining 2 tablespoons (25 g) of sugar. Mix to blend and set aside. Spread the filling over the dough rectangle instead of the cinnamon filling. Finish the recipe as directed.

Patience

Cover the dough and let it rest in a warm (75°F, or 24°C) place for 3 to 4 hours.

Perform a couple of stretches and folds (see page 40) during the warm fermentation process to add more strength to the dough. The dough should become puffy and almost double in volume.

To make the filling: In a small bowl, stir together all the filling ingredients until combined and set aside.

To make the icing: In a medium-size bowl and using a handheld mixer, beat all the icing ingredients until light and fluffy. Set aside, or refrigerate, until needed.

To make the buns: Line a 9 × 13-inch (23 × 33 cm) baking dish with parchment paper. Flour a work surface and turn the dough onto it.

Fun Part

Using a rolling pin, roll the dough into a 15 × 20-inch (38 × 50 cm) rectangle. Use a spoon or your hands to spread the filling evenly over the dough. Starting with a long end nearest you, roll the dough into a log. Cut the log into 2-inch (5 cm) slices and place them in the prepared baking dish, cut-side down. Cover the dish and let the buns rise in a warm (75°F, or 24°C) place for 2 to 3 hours until they're puffy.

If you'd like to bake the buns the next day: Move the proofed buns into the refrigerator overnight, and bake the buns the next day following the directions as listed and removing the pan from the refrigerator to let the buns warm up, covered, while the oven preheats. Remove the cover before baking.

If you'd like to bake the buns immediately: Ask an adult to preheat the oven to 400°F (200°C).

Remove the cover from the baking dish. Ask an adult to place the buns in the oven and bake the cinnamon buns for about 20 minutes until golden (they may need a few more minutes if they've been refrigerated overnight). Ask an adult to help you remove the hot pan from the oven. Let cool for 5 to 10 minutes before icing.

Ice the cooled cinnamon rolls with the delicious cream cheese icing you made.

Sample Schedule

After making the starter the evening before baking the cinnamon buns, you will need 8 hours plus about 45 minutes to preheat the oven and bake the buns on Day 2 to finish the recipe.

	DAY 1	DAY 2
Make the cinnamon buns starter	Evening	
Combine the ingredients (except salt and butter)		9:00 a.m.
Add salt and butter; let rest (including 2 stretch/folds)		10:00 a.m.
Make the filling and icings		1:00 p.m.
Roll the dough, add filling, and slice		2:00 p.m.
Bake		5:00 p.m. (or next morning after refrigerating overnight)

BREADCRUMBS

Cinnamon buns are called different names throughout the world. In Sweden, they are known as "kanelbulle." Other places refer to them as cinnamon rolls, sticky rolls, and sticky buns. Cinnamon is one of the oldest spices in the world, dating back to biblical times. Ancient Egyptians used cinnamon to flavor food and drinks and it also had several medicinal purposes. It was so highly treasured it was considered more precious than gold.

CHAPTER 5

SAVORY RECIPES
MADE FROM SOURDOUGH DISCARD

• ● •

You've learned everything you need to know about sourdough bread and sourdough starter. And now, you have so much sourdough discard left sitting inside your refrigerator. What should you do with it? Let's turn it into something delicious. In the next two chapters, I'll show you how to use sourdough starter discard in the most familiar but unusually delicious recipes—from pancakes and English muffins to crackers, brownies, and banana bread.

BREADCRUMBS

Fun fact! English muffins are not baked, they're griddled. They never see an oven.

English Muffins

**8 to 10
English muffins,
depending on size**

3 tablespoons plus
2 teaspoons (55 g)
lukewarm (100°F or 38°C)
filtered water

6 tablespoons plus
1 teaspoon (95 g) lukewarm
(100°F or 38°C) milk

Scant ¼ teaspoon (0.5 g)
active dry yeast (optional;
to speed up the process)

½ cup (130 g) sourdough
starter discard (see
page 32)

1 heaping tablespoon
(15 g) sugar

1 heaping teaspoon
(7 g) salt

2¼ cups (281 g) unbleached
all-purpose flour, plus
3 to 4 tablespoons (23 to
31 g) and more for dusting,
as needed

2 tablespoons (28 g) canola
or vegetable oil

Corn flour, for dusting

What comes to mind when you hear the words "English muffins"? English muffins are very versatile. I associate them with a perfect egg, ham, and cheese sandwich. For my kids, it's a small English muffin pizza or French toast. This recipe is very easy, and includes the most incredible thing—sourdough discard. Let's get started.

Ask an adult to set up a stand mixer fitted with the dough hook attachment. Add the lukewarm water and milk to the bowl, along with the yeast, if using. Stir in the sourdough starter discard until dissolved.

Add the sugar, salt, and 2¼ cups (281 g) of flour. Mix on medium speed for 5 to 10 minutes until the dough comes together and is smooth. Add the oil and continue mixing for 2 minutes until well incorporated.

Note: Once you add the oil, if the dough seems too sticky, incorporate the extra 3 to 4 tablespoons (23 to 31 g) of flour.

Cover the bowl with a plastic wrap and let the dough proof for about 4 hours in a warm (75°F, or 24°C) place until doubled in size and puffy.

Fun Part

Dust a work surface with all-purpose flour and turn the dough onto it. Flatten the dough with your hands. Using a rolling pin, roll the dough to about ½ inch (1 cm) thick.

Dust a baking sheet with corn flour.

Using a 3-inch (7.5 cm) biscuit cutter or a glass with a thin rim, cut out dough circles and place them on the prepared baking sheet. Cover with plastic wrap.

CONTINUED

Sample Schedule
You should be able to complete this recipe in about 2 hours.

	DAY 1
Mix ingredients and proof	9:00 a.m.
Roll out dough, cut circles, and proof	1:00 p.m.
Heat pan and cook	3:00 p.m.

Patience

Set the English muffins in a warm (75°F, or 24°C) place for about 2 hours until the muffins are bigger and puffy.

Ask an adult to place a cast-iron or stainless-steel skillet over medium heat on the stovetop until it is very hot. Reduce the heat to medium-low and add the English muffins, working in batches as needed. Cook for 4 to 6 minutes per side until golden brown and cooked all the way through. Let cool for 10 to 15 minutes. Enjoy!

✦ Tip

For storing, let the English muffins cool, then transfer them to an airtight bag. Refrigerate for up to 2 weeks, or freeze for up to 2 months. Split the muffins before toasting.

✶ DELICIOUS IDEAS ✶

ENGLISH MUFFIN FRENCH TOAST

> 6 English muffins
>
> 1 large egg
>
> ½ cup (120 g) milk
>
> 2 tablespoons (25 g) sugar
>
> 1 teaspoon (4.3 g) vanilla extract
>
> ½ teaspoon (1.5 g) ground cinnamon
>
> 2 tablespoons (28 g) butter

Ask a parent or other trusted adult to help you cut each English muffin in half horizontally.

In a medium-size bowl, whisk the egg, milk, sugar, vanilla, and cinnamon until blended.

Ask an adult to place a skillet on the stovetop over medium heat. Add the butter to the skillet to melt.

Dip each English muffin half into the egg mixture. Ask an adult to supervise while you transfer the English muffins to the hot skillet. You will need to work in batches. Cook the muffins for 2 to 3 minutes, then flip them over. Cook for 2 to 3 minutes more until golden brown.

GRILLED CHEESE ENGLISH MUFFIN PANINI

Panini is the Italian word for "sandwich." They're grilled in a special panini press, which makes it crispy on the outside and gooey on the inside. If you don't have one, use a skillet instead.

> 1 English muffin
>
> 2 slices cheese of choice (American, Cheddar, or mozzarella)

Ask an adult to help cut the English muffin in half horizontally. Put 2 slices of cheese on one half and top with the second half, like a sandwich.

Ask an adult to preheat a panini press to medium heat. Alternatively, place a cast-iron skillet over medium heat to preheat. Place your panini in the press, close the lid, and cook for 2 to 3 minutes. If you are using a skillet, press down on the sandwich with a spatula to flatten it.

Ask an adult to remove the lid and flip the panini to the other side. Close the lid and cook for 2 minutes more, until the cheese melts.

Sourdough Biscuits

8 to 12 biscuits, depending on size

1½ cups (187 g) unbleached all-purpose flour, plus more as needed

½ cup (60 g) whole wheat, whole grain flour

1 tablespoon (12.5 g) sugar

1 teaspoon (6 g) salt

1 teaspoon (4 g) baking powder

½ teaspoon (2 g) baking soda

1 stick (120 g) cold butter

½ cup (115 g) nonfat Greek yogurt, plus more as needed

1 cup (260 g) sourdough starter discard (see page 32)

BREADCRUMBS

In the United Kingdom, if you ask for a biscuit, you'll get what Americans know as a cookie. And, if you ask for a biscuit in the United States, you'll get what the English know as scones.

Biscuits make a delicious breakfast. Bigger biscuits are perfect for breakfast sandwiches. They can be paired with egg, avocado, and any protein you choose. Biscuits also taste great with butter and jam. These biscuits use sourdough starter discard in the recipe. Plus, I like to use a combination of all-purpose and whole wheat, whole grain flour for a healthy biscuit.

Ask an adult to set up a food processor with the mixing blade and supervise the next steps. In the food processor, combine the flours, sugar, salt, baking powder, baking soda, and cold butter. Pulse until coarse crumbs form.

Add the yogurt and sourdough starter discard. Mix well until a lumpy dough forms.

Note: If your biscuit dough seems very dry, add a bit more yogurt until it comes together. If your biscuit dough seems too loose, add a little more flour.

Ask an adult to preheat the oven to 400°F (200°C). Line a baking sheet with parchment paper.

Fun Part
Dust a work surface with flour and have an adult carefully transfer the dough on top. Using a rolling pin, roll the dough ¾ to 1 inch (2 to 2.5 cm) thick.

Using a 2-inch (5 cm) biscuit cutter or a glass, cut 8 to 10 rounds from the dough. Cut the biscuits as close together as possible. Collect all the dough scraps, pat them together, roll it again to 1 inch (2.5 cm) thick, and cut more biscuits.

Place each biscuit on the prepared baking sheet about 2 inches (5 cm) apart because they will spread during baking.

Ask an adult to place the baking sheet into the hot oven. Bake for 15 to 20 minutes until golden brown. Ask an adult to remove the biscuits from the hot oven and serve warm.

Note: The biscuits can be stored in an airtight bag or container at room temperature for about 2 days. To keep them fresh longer, put a slice of bread into the bag to absorb moisture.

Sample Schedule
There are no long stretches of time required for this recipe.

✴ DELICIOUS IDEAS ✴

For added flavor, mix in some chopped fresh chives, dill, or scallions; or use garlic butter instead of plain butter.

Cheddar Scones

1 to 2 dozen, depending on size

2 cups (250 g) unbleached all-purpose flour, plus 4 to 5 tablespoons (31 to 39 g) if needed, plus more for dusting

2 tablespoons (25 g) sugar

1 teaspoon (4 g) baking powder

½ teaspoon (4 g) baking soda

½ teaspoon (3 g) salt

1 stick (120 g) cold butter

1 cup (116 g) grated sharp Cheddar cheese

½ cup (130 g) cold sourdough starter discard (see page 32)

6 tablespoons plus 2 teaspoons (100 g) buttermilk

1 large egg

1 teaspoon (6 g) Dijon mustard (optional)

Cheesy scones were a new discovery for me. I was having people over for brunch and wanted to surprise them with something new and delicious. In my search for ideas, this cheesy scone recipe came to my attention. And, oh my, it is an absolute winner. And I added my secret ingredient—sourdough starter discard.

Ask an adult to set up a food processor with the mixing blade and supervise the next steps. In the food processor, combine the flour, sugar, baking powder, baking soda, salt, and cold butter. Pulse until coarse crumbs form. Have an adult carefully transfer the crumbs to a medium-size bowl; whisk in the cheese.

In another medium-size bowl, stir together the cold sourdough starter discard, buttermilk, egg, and mustard (if using). Add the liquid ingredients to the dry ingredients and mix until a lumpy dough forms. Cover the dough with plastic wrap and refrigerate for 30 minutes to 1 hour.

Ask an adult to preheat the oven to 400°F (200°C). Line a baking sheet with parchment paper.

Fun Part

Generously dust a work surface with flour and place the cold dough on it. Using a rolling pin, roll the dough 1 inch (2.5 cm) thick. Cut the dough as you want—into squares, circles, or wedges 2 to 3 inches (5 to 7.5 cm) across. Transfer the scones to the prepared baking sheet, leaving some space between them because they will grow bigger in the oven.

Ask a parent or other trusted adult to place the baking sheet into the hot oven. Bake for 15 to 20 minutes until the scones are golden with slightly brown edges. Ask an adult to remove the hot scones from the oven. Let the scones cool for 5 to 10 minutes. Enjoy.

Note: Store the scones in an airtight bag or container at room temperature for about 2 days. To keep them fresh longer, put a slice of bread into the bag to absorb moisture.

Sample Schedule
You should be able to complete this recipe in about 2 hours.

	DAY 1
Mix ingredients and refrigerate	12 p.m.
Roll, cut, and bake	1 p.m.

Tortillas

Tortillas can be great for breakfast, lunch, or dinner and also for a snack. Using sourdough starter discard in this recipe makes tortillas more delicious and easily digestible.

6 tortillas

1 cup (125 g) unbleached all-purpose flour, plus more for dusting

Scant ⅔ cup (75 g) whole wheat, whole grain flour

2 teaspoons (10 g) sugar

½ teaspoon (3 g) salt

¼ teaspoon (1 g) baking powder (optional, to lower acidity)

2 tablespoons (30 g) cold butter

½ cup (130 g) sourdough starter discard (see page 32)

¼ cup plus 2 teaspoons (70 g) filtered water

Ask an adult to set up a food processor with the mixing blade and supervise the next steps. In the food processor, mix the flours, sugar, salt, and baking powder (if using). Add the cold butter and pulse until coarse crumbs form. Little by little, add the starter and water (you might not need all the water) and mix to combine.

Dust a work surface with flour and have an adult carefully transfer the dough on top. Knead until a soft dough forms.

Patience
Wrap the dough in plastic wrap and let it rest at room temperature for 2 to 3 hours.

Note: By the end of the resting time, the dough will become bigger and puffy.

Fun Part
Divide the dough into 6 equal parts. Round each piece of dough, press it down, and use a rolling pin to roll it into disk-shaped tortillas as thin as possible, about ⅙ inch (4 mm) thin (you don't want your tortillas to be thick).

Ask an adult to place a cast-iron skillet on the stovetop over medium-high heat until very hot. Carefully place a tortilla in the hot skillet and cook for 1 to 2 minutes per side until large bubbles form. Remove the cooked tortilla and repeat the process with the remaining tortillas.

While still warm, cover the tortillas with plastic wrap; the steam will soften them. For storing, place the tortillas in an airtight bag and refrigerate for up to 1 week.

BREADCRUMBS

The word *tortilla* comes from the Spanish word *torta*, which means round cake, and the diminutive *illa*. So a tortilla is a "little cake." What will you fill your tortillas with?

Sample Schedule
To prepare this recipe you'll need at least 2 to 3 hours.

	DAY 1
Mix ingredients and proof	9 a.m.
Cut, roll, shape, and cook	11 a.m.

CINNAMON TORTILLAS

1 teaspoon (3 g) ground
cinnamon

2 tablespoons (25 g) sugar

Freshly cooked tortillas

Melted butter, for spreading

In a small bowl, stir together the cinnamon and sugar.

Place the tortillas on a work surface and brush them with melted butter, then sprinkle with the cinnamon-sugar mixture. Microwave the tortillas on medium power for 40 seconds. Cut into triangles and serve.

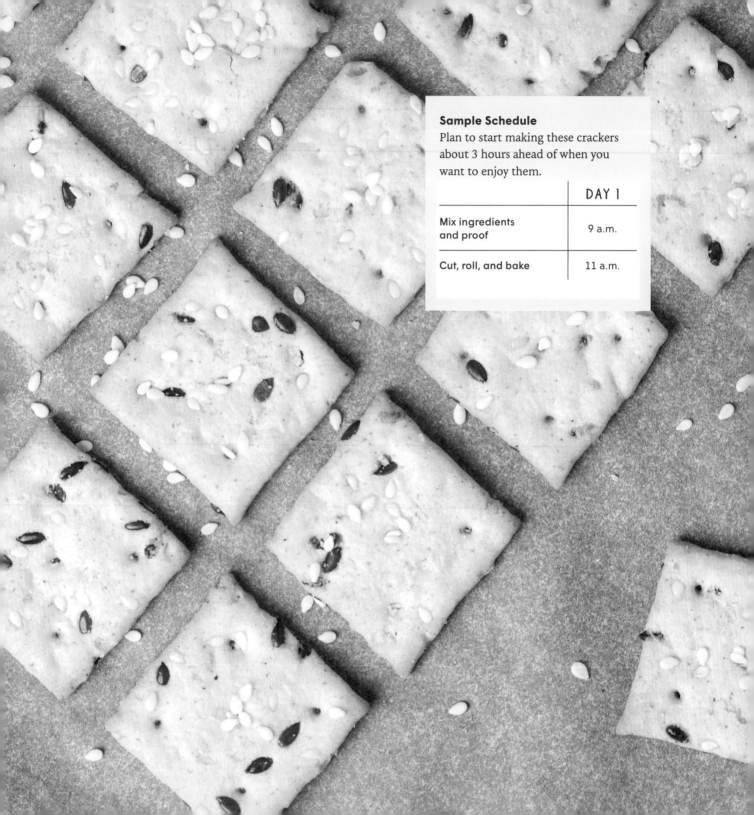

Sourdough Crackers

**2 trays
of crackers**

¾ cup plus 1 tablespoon plus 1 teaspoon (100 g) whole wheat, whole grain flour

½ teaspoon (2 g) sugar

½ teaspoon (3 g) salt

2 tablespoons (30 g) cold butter

1 tablespoon plus 2 teaspoons (20 g) flaxseed or flax meal, or any seeds you like

⅓ cup (40 g) your favorite shredded cheese (Parmesan or Cheddar is delicious)

1 cup minus 3 tablespoons (210 g) sourdough starter discard (see page 32)

Sourdough crackers are another good way to use sourdough starter discard while also enjoying a healthy and delicious snack. Serve the crackers with your favorite cheese plate, or have them with any dipping sauce or hummus, or eat as a snack with carrots and apples just as they are. To spruce up the recipe, add different herbs, cheeses, or seeds.

Ask an adult to set up a food processor with the mixing blade and supervise the next steps. In the food processor, combine the flour, sugar, salt, cold butter, flaxseed, and cheese. Pulse until medium-coarse crumbs form. Have an adult carefully transfer the crumbs to a medium-size bowl; add the sourdough starter discard. Use your hands or a spatula to mix and incorporate the ingredients together.

Patience
Form the dough into a ball, cover it with plastic wrap, and move it to the refrigerator for 2 hours.

Ask an adult to preheat the oven 350°F (180°C). Prepare 2 sheets of parchment paper, about the size of the baking sheets you will use.

Divide the dough into 2 equal pieces, which will make rolling easier.

Fun Part
Put one piece of dough on the first sheet of parchment, then cover it with the second sheet of parchment. Using a rolling pin, roll on top of the paper in all directions to make the dough thin. Flip the dough trapped between the paper sheets and roll on the other side of the paper too, until the dough becomes as thin as possible, about ⅛ inch (3 mm) thin.

Carefully remove the top sheet of parchment from the dough and ask an adult to help you cut the crackers. They can be square, rectangular, or long strips. Carefully transfer the parchment paper with the crackers to a baking sheet and repeat with the second piece of dough, using a new piece of parchment paper.

Ask a parent or other trusted adult to place the baking sheet into the hot oven. Bake the crackers for 15 to 20 minutes until golden. Ask an adult to remove the hot crackers from the oven. Let the crackers cool completely to become crunchy. I like to store the crackers in a jar with a tightly closed lid, or an airtight bag will work, too.

Sourdough Popovers

10 to 12 popovers

3 large eggs, at room temperature

1 cup minus 1 tablespoon (225 g) lukewarm (100°F or 38°C) milk

½ cup (130 g) sourdough starter discard (see page 32)

½ teaspoon (3 g) salt

2 scant teaspoons (9 g) sugar

1¼ cups (156 g) unbleached all-purpose flour

Melted butter, for the muffin tin

Popovers are very versatile. They can be eaten with all kinds of toppings, sweet or savory, or just with butter. In England, popovers are usually served with a dinner roast. But the American version is usually served as a sweet addition to breakfast or brunch. Popovers are simple to make, plus we can use our sourdough starter discard in the recipe.

Remove the eggs from the refrigerator a couple of hours before making the dough to come to room temperature.

Place a 12-count muffin tin inside the oven and ask an adult to preheat the oven to 450°F (230°C).

In a large bowl, whisk the eggs, milk, sourdough starter discard, salt, and sugar until all the sourdough starter dissolves.

Whisk in the flour, but be gentle—don't overmix the batter. It should be slightly runny. Transfer the batter to a large pitcher.

Ask an adult to remove the hot muffin tin from the oven. Brush each muffin mold with melted butter and put the muffin tin back into the oven for 1 minute, so it will be very hot (ask an adult to help).

Ask an adult to remove the hot muffin tin from the oven again and pour the batter into the buttered molds, filling each about three-fourths full. Move fast but be careful.

Note: If you'd like taller popovers, use a muffin tin for taller muffins or use a popover pan.

Ask a parent or other trusted adult to place the muffin tin into the hot oven. Bake for 15 minutes. Ask an adult to lower the oven temperature to 350°F (180°C) and bake the popovers for 10 minutes more until they are puffy and golden brown. Ask an adult to remove the tin from the oven and flip the tin over so the muffins come out. Serve immediately.

Sample Schedule
There are no long stretches of time required for this recipe.

✱ DELICIOUS IDEAS ✱

In addition to the delicious ideas here, you can also serve popovers with butter and your favorite jam, or serve them for dinner to dip in a savory gravy.

For cinnamon popovers: Brush the baked popovers with melted butter, then roll them in a mixture of sugar and cinnamon.

For powdered sugar popovers: Let the baked popovers cool, then roll in powdered sugar.

Add a chocolate glaze: In a medium-size microwave-safe bowl, stir together ½ cup (88 g) chocolate chips, 2 tablespoons (30 g) butter, 2 teaspoons (14 g) honey, and 2 teaspoons (10 g) water. Ask an adult to microwave it on high power for 20 seconds, stir, and microwave for a couple seconds more until melted and smooth. Dip the top of each popover into the chocolate glaze. You can add some sprinkles, too.

Or, add a white icing: In a medium-size bowl, stir together ½ cup (60 g) powdered sugar and 2 to 3 tablespoons (30 to 45 g) milk until you get an even, spreadable consistency. Dip each popover into the glaze and add some sprinkles on top.

CHAPTER 6

SWEET TREATS AND DESSERTS

MADE WITH SOURDOUGH DISCARD

• • • •

Desserts made with sourdough discard taste so much better than those without it and are a lot softer and moister. In this chapter, I share the best sweet treats approved by the toughest judges—my kids. I know these will soon be your family's favorites, too.

Banana Bread

10 to 12 slices

Butter, for coating the loaf pan

2 cups (240 g) unbleached all-purpose flour, plus more for the loaf pan

3 ripe bananas

⅔ cup (150 g) light brown sugar

⅓ cup plus 2 teaspoons (90 g) canola or vegetable oil

½ cup plus 1 tablespoon plus ¾ teaspoon (150 g) sourdough starter discard (see page 32)

2 large eggs

1 teaspoon (4.3 g) vanilla extract

1½ teaspoons (6 g) baking soda

1 teaspoon (3 g) ground cinnamon

¼ teaspoon (1.5 g) salt

½ cup chocolate chips (88 g; optional) or chopped walnuts (50 g; optional)

Banana bread has a special place in my heart. The first time I tried it was when my husband and I moved to the United States from Ukraine. Bananas were such a rare treat when I was a child because my mom would buy them only on holidays. Since then, it's become one of my favorite fruits. And, of course, banana bread is a favorite treat for my kids. Sourdough starter discard makes the banana bread even better—super-moist, super-soft, and super-simple to make.

Ask an adult to preheat the oven to 350°F (180°C). Coat a 9 × 5-inch (23 × 13 cm) loaf pan with butter and sprinkle it with flour, knocking out the excess, to prevent sticking. Set aside.

Ask an adult to set up a stand mixer fitted with the paddle attachment.

Peel the bananas and use a fork to mash them on a plate. Put the mashed bananas in the mixer's bowl and add the brown sugar, oil, sourdough starter discard, eggs, and vanilla. Mix on low speed for 2 to 3 minutes until everything is well incorporated.

Stop the mixer and add the flour, baking soda, cinnamon, and salt. Mix on low speed for 1 to 2 minutes, until well incorporated. Add the chocolate chips (if using) or walnuts (if using) at the end of mixing. Pour the batter into the prepared loaf pan.

Transfer the loaf pan to a baking sheet and ask an adult to place it into the hot oven. Bake for 55 to 60 minutes until golden brown. Ask an adult to check for doneness by pressing the top of the banana bread.

If it bounces back, the loaf is ready. If it remains indented, give it 5 to 10 minutes more in the oven. An adult should remove the loaf pan from the hot oven. Let the loaf cool in the pan for 1 hour and then remove it from the pan and let it cool for another 20 to 30 minutes.

+ **Tip**

Prepare the batter the night before and leave it in the refrigerator overnight. This will give the batter time to ferment and give the loaf a tangy flavor.

Sample Schedule

There are no long stretches of time required for this recipe.

Blueberry Muffins

12 to 18 muffins, depending on size

8 tablespoons (1 stick; 113 g) butter, at room temperature

⅔ cup (130 g) granulated sugar, plus more for sprinkling

7 tablespoons plus 1 teaspoon (100 g) light brown sugar

2 large eggs, at room temperature

1 teaspoon (4.3 g) vanilla extract

½ cup (130 g) sourdough starter discard (see page 32)

¾ cup (160 g) sour cream, plus more as needed

2⅓ cups (290 g) unbleached all-purpose flour, plus more as needed

1½ teaspoons (6 g) baking soda

Heaping ½ teaspoon (4 g) salt

2 cups (290 g) fresh or (310 g) frozen blueberries

It never ceases to amaze me how excited my kids get when we bake a batch of muffins. We change the fillings—from blueberry to cinnamon crumb to chocolate chips, cranberry, s'mores, or just plain vanilla—and each time, it's a success. This is my go-to recipe for delicious blueberry muffins made with sourdough starter discard for extra softness.

Ask an adult to preheat the oven to 350°F (180°C).

Prepare a muffin tin with paper muffin liners.

Ask an adult to set up a stand mixer fitted with the paddle attachment. Add the butter, granulated sugar, and brown sugar to the bowl and mix on medium speed until the ingredients become lighter and airier.

One at a time, add the eggs and mix well after each addition. Add the vanilla and sourdough starter discard. Mix until the discard is well incorporated into the batter. Add the sour cream and mix for about 2 minutes.

Meanwhile, in a medium-size bowl, stir together the flour, baking soda, and salt. Add the dry ingredients to the wet ingredients and mix on low speed until the flour is well incorporated.

Note: The batter should be thick—not runny—and not dry or extra-thick like dough. If the batter is too runny, add more flour, 1 tablespoon (7.5 g) at a time, until the batter reaches the correct consistency. If the batter is dry or too thick, add a little more sour cream, 1 tablespoon (14 g) at a time until the proper consistency is reached.

Use a spatula to fold the blueberries into the batter.

Fun Part

Use an ice cream scooper, or tablespoon, to fill the molds of the muffin tin about three-fourths full of batter. Sprinkle a little granulated sugar on top of each muffin.

Ask an adult to place the muffin tin into the hot oven. Bake for 30 minutes until slightly brown. Ask an adult to test for doneness by inserting a toothpick into the center of a muffin. If it comes out clean or with a few crumbs attached, your muffins are done. Ask an adult to remove the hot muffin tin from the oven. Let them cool and enjoy.

Sample Schedule
There are no long stretches of time required for this recipe.

BREADCRUMBS

Blueberries are super-healthy fruits—in fact, they're even considered a "superfood," packed with vitamins and antioxidants, which help fight disease. So don't be shy about popping a few extra blueberries in your mouth as you make this recipe!

Crumpets

12 to 14 crumpets

If you like pancakes but are tired of eating them every weekend morning, try these crumpets to change up your breakfast routine. Serve the crumpets warm with butter, jam, honey, or maple syrup.

½ cup minus 1 teaspoon (115 g) lukewarm (100°F or 38°C) milk

2 tablespoons plus 2 teaspoons (35 g) sugar

Heaping ½ teaspoon (4 g) salt

1 cup (260 g) sourdough starter discard (see page 32)

Scant ½ cup (60 g) unbleached all-purpose flour

1½ teaspoons (6 g) baking soda

Butter or oil, to coat the skillet

In a medium-size bowl, stir together the lukewarm milk, sugar, and salt. Whisk in the sourdough starter discard until everything is combined and the discard dissolves.

In a small bowl, stir together the flour and baking soda. Add the dry ingredients to the liquid mixture and whisk until no lumps remain.

Patience

Cover the bowl and let the batter rest for 15 minutes.

Observe

The dough will become very bubbly and puffy as the baking soda reacts with the acids from the sourdough starter discard.

Ask an adult to preheat a skillet over medium-low heat until hot. Using a pastry brush, coat the skillet with butter. With an adult helping, using a tablespoon, pour the batter into the hot skillet; try to make the crumpets round.

Note: Don't pour more than 4 crumpets into the hot skillet at once; space between them makes flipping easier.

Cook the crumpets for 1 to 2 minutes. The batter will begin to rise and bubble on top. Flip the crumpets and cook for 1 to 2 minutes more until both sides are golden brown. Serve hot, topped as desired.

Sample Schedule

With only 7 ingredients and 15 minutes of patience, you'll be eating crumpets in no time with this recipe.

	DAY 1
Mix ingredients, cover, and rest	8:00 a.m.
Cook	8:15 a.m.

CRUMPETS WITH CARAMELIZED BANANAS

¼ cup (55 g) light brown sugar

2 tablespoons (30 g) filtered water

3 bananas, thickly sliced on the diagonal

½ cup (120 g) heavy whipping cream

¼ cup (50 g) granulated sugar

Ask an adult to help with all the steps here. In a medium-size skillet over medium heat, combine the brown sugar and water. Cook, stirring, for 2 minutes, or until the brown sugar dissolves. Increase the heat to medium-high and bring the liquid to a boil.

Add the banana slices. Cook for 2 minutes, gently turning the bananas, or until the sauce thickens and the bananas are well coated.

Pour the heavy whipping cream into a 16-ounce (480 ml) jar and add the granulated sugar. Tightly close the lid and shake the jar as hard as you can. As soon as the cream becomes thicker, continue shaking but with less intensity. Stop when the cream is whipped (when it reaches stiff peaks).

Serve the hot crumpets topped with the caramelized bananas and whipped cream.

Pancakes

12 to 18 small pancakes

Pancakes are another great way to use sourdough starter discard. This is a delicious weekend treat that's like dessert for breakfast that will satisfy a happy family. This recipe was approved by many of my friends, and they all fell in love with it, as I know you will, too.

SPONGE

1 cup minus 2 scant tablespoons (230 g) sourdough starter discard (see page 32)

1 cup plus 2 teaspoons (250 g) buttermilk

1 cup (125 g) unbleached all-purpose flour

BATTER

1 recipe sponge

2 large eggs

6 tablespoons (75 g) sugar

Heaping ½ teaspoon (4 g) salt

1 teaspoon (4.3 g) vanilla extract

1 tablespoon plus 1 teaspoon (19 g) butter, melted, plus more for the skillet

1 teaspoon (4 g) baking soda

½ cup (60 g) whole wheat, whole grain flour

To make the sponge: Prepare the sponge the night before. In a medium-size bowl, stir together the sourdough starter discard, buttermilk, and all-purpose flour until well blended. Cover and let ferment overnight at room temperature.

In the morning, you'll find the sponge full of bubbles from the fermentation.

To make the batter: Add the eggs, sugar, salt, and vanilla to the sponge and mix it very well. Stir in the melted butter. Stir in the baking soda and whole wheat, whole grain flour until blended.

Patience

Cover the batter and let rest for 15 minutes. It should get bigger.

Observe

Baking soda will react with the acids from the sourdough starter discard, releasing carbon dioxide (CO_2). This reaction will make the pancakes puffy and light.

Note: The pancakes can be made without baking soda, but you'll have to mix all ingredients for the sponge and batter together and let the batter ferment in the refrigerator overnight. The pancakes will have a tangy flavor from the discard—the baking soda lowers the acidity and makes them less tangy.

Ask an adult to turn the stovetop to medium-low heat. Coat a large skillet with butter and place it over the heat to preheat until hot. Using a spoon and with an adult's help, pour the batter into the hot skillet. Try to make the pancakes round.

Note: Don't pour more than 4 pancakes into a big skillet at once; leaving space between them makes flipping easier.

Cook the pancakes for 1 to 2 minutes. The batter will begin to rise and bubble on top. Flip the pancakes over and cook for 1 to 2 minutes more until both sides are golden brown. Serve the pancakes immediately with your favorite toppings.

CONTINUED

Sample Schedule

After making the sponge the evening before, you'll need only about 1 hour to get these delicious pancakes on your plate.

	DAY 1	DAY 2
Prepare sponge	Evening	
Mix ingredients, cover, and let rest		8:00 a.m.
Cook		8:15 a.m.

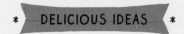

* DELICIOUS IDEAS *

PANCAKES WITH TART CHERRY SAUCE AND WHIPPED CREAM

2 cups (280 g) frozen tart cherries

1 cup (200 g) sugar plus ¼ cup (50 g)

1 tablespoon plus ¾ teaspoon (10 g) cornstarch

½ cup (120 g) heavy whipping cream

With an adult's help, put the frozen cherries in a medium-size saucepan over medium heat. Remove 2 tablespoons (25 g) of sugar from the 1 cup (200 g) of sugar and set aside. Add the remaining sugar from the 1 cup to the cherries and cook, stirring, until the cherries thaw, about 5 minutes.

In a small bowl, whisk the reserved 2 tablespoons (25 g) of sugar with 1 tablespoon of the cornstarch to blend and add to the cherries. Cook, while stirring, until the sauce becomes thicker but is still runny, about 5 minutes.

Pour the heavy whipping cream into a 16-ounce (480 ml) jar and add the remaining ¼ cup (50 g) of sugar. Tightly close the lid and shake the jar as hard as you can. As soon as the cream becomes thicker, continue shaking but with less intensity. Stop when the cream is whipped (when it reaches stiff peaks).

Serve the hot pancakes topped with warm cherry sauce and whipped cream.

Apple Galette

My friend Nadya shared this recipe with me more than ten years ago. It's become my go-to dough for galette or piecrust. The dough is flaky, airy, and delicious (and made even more so with the inclusion of the sourdough starter discard). Also, it doesn't get mushy from the fruit juices during baking.

DOUGH

2 cups (250 g) unbleached all-purpose flour, plus more for dusting

2 sticks (226 g) cold butter

½ teaspoon (3 g) salt

2 tablespoons (40 g) sour cream

2 large egg yolks

½ cup (130 g) sourdough starter discard (see page 32)

APPLE FILLING

6 to 8 medium-size apples (Granny Smith and a mix of sweet apples)

½ cup (110 g) light brown sugar

1 tablespoon (7.8 g) all-purpose flour

1 teaspoon (4.3 g) vanilla extract

1 teaspoon (3 g) ground cinnamon

¼ teaspoon (1.5 g) salt

Granulated sugar, for sprinkling

1 tablespoons plus 1 teaspoon (20 g) cold butter, cubed

Vanilla ice cream, for serving

To make the dough: Ask an adult to set up a food processor with the mixing blade and supervise the next steps. In the food processor, combine the flour, cold butter, and salt. Pulse until coarse crumbs form. Add the sour cream, egg yolks, and sourdough starter discard. Process until a dough forms but is lumpy.

Ask an adult to dump the dough onto a work surface; gather it into a ball. Cover the dough with plastic wrap and refrigerate for at least 1 hour.

Note: The dough can be frozen for up to 1 month.

To make the filling: Meanwhile, ask an adult to help you peel, core, and cut the apples into ⅛-inch (3 mm)-thick slices and place them in a bowl. Add the brown sugar, flour, vanilla, cinnamon, and salt. Stir everything together to mix and coat the apples. Set aside.

Ask an adult to preheat the oven to 350°F (180°C). Line a baking sheet with parchment paper.

To make the galette: Remove the dough from the refrigerator. Dust a work surface with flour and place the dough on it. Using a rolling pin, roll the dough into a thin 12- to 15-inch (30 to 37.5 cm) circle about ⅛ inch (3 mm) thick. The edges can be rough because you will fold them anyway.

Note: For easier rolling, sprinkle the top of the dough with flour and flip it to the opposite side to continue rolling.

Transfer the dough to the prepared baking sheet. Spread the filling inside the dough circle, arranging the apple slices into any pattern you like. I like overlapping concentric circles. Leave a 3-inch (7.5 cm) border around the edge without any filling. Fold the edges of the dough over, pleating and pinching it to form a crust. If the dough tears, patch it by pinching some dough from the edges.

Brush the top of the dough with water and sprinkle it with granulated sugar. Dot the galette filling with the butter cubes. The sugar and butter will caramelize during baking and will give you a delicious result.

CONTINUED

Ask an adult to put the galette into the hot oven. Bake for 55 to 60 minutes until golden brown and bubbling. Ask an adult to remove the galette from the hot oven. Let cool for 5 to 10 minutes, and serve warm with a scoop of vanilla ice cream.

✦ Tip

After 30 minutes of baking, cover the top of the galette with aluminum foil, which will help the apples cook through and keep the edges of the galette from burning. Remove the foil for the final 10 minutes of baking.

Sample Schedule

With only 2 hours between mixing and baking, this recipe can be made on a whim.

	DAY 1
Mix dough ingredients and refrigerate	2:00 p.m.
Form galette and bake	4:00 p.m.

✴ DELICIOUS IDEAS ✴

This dough can be used to make a perfect piecrust. The galette can also be filled with seasonal fruits: apricots, blueberries, cherries peaches, plums . . . just mix them with sugar and flour, following the directions for the apples, and you'll be delighted with the delicious results.

BREADCRUMBS

Galette is a type of dessert made with a rustic, free-form crust. It's a kind of dish-free pie.

Cinnamon Crumb Coffee Cake

10 to 12 slices

This is my mom's famous coffee cake recipe. She uses jam as a filling, but I prefer blueberries or apples. It's great as a breakfast or dessert, or with a cup of afternoon tea.

STREUSEL

½ cup plus 2 tablespoons plus 1 teaspoon (80 g) unbleached all-purpose flour

½ cup (100 g) sugar

¼ cup (30 g) chopped pecans (optional)

1 teaspoon (3 g) ground cinnamon

½ teaspoon (3 g) salt

4 tablespoons (½ stick; 60 g) cold butter

COFFEE CAKE

8 tablespoons (1 stick; 113 g) butter, at room temperature, plus more for coating the pan

1 cup plus 3½ tablespoons sugar (245 g)

1 large egg

1 teaspoon (4.3 g) vanilla extract

½ cup plus 1 tablespoon plus ¾ teaspoon (150 g) sourdough starter discard (see page 32)

1 cup (220 g) sour cream

2 cups plus scant ½ cup (300 g) unbleached all-purpose flour

1 teaspoon (4 g) baking powder

½ teaspoon (2 g) baking soda

½ teaspoon (3 g) salt

FILLING (OPTIONAL)

1 cup (145 g) fresh blueberries or 1 cup (150 g) diced apple

To make the streusel: Ask an adult to set up a food processor with the mixing blade and supervise the next steps. In the food processor, combine the flour, sugar, pecans (if using), cinnamon, and salt. Add the cold butter and pulse until coarse crumbs form. Ask an adult to carefully transfer the streusel to a bowl. Set aside.

To make the coffee cake: Ask an adult to preheat the oven to 350°F (180°C). Lightly coat an 9-inch (23 cm) square or round baking pan with butter.

Ask an adult to set up a stand mixer fitted with the paddle attachment. Put the room-temperature butter and sugar into the bowl and mix until creamy. Add the egg, vanilla, sourdough starter discard, and sour cream. Mix on low speed until well combined. Add the flour, baking powder, baking soda, and salt. Mix until well combined. The dough will look firm, not liquid. Spread half the batter into the prepared pan.

Sprinkle half the streusel on top.

Sample Schedule
There are no long stretches of
time required for this recipe.

To fill the coffee cake: Spread the blueberries (if using) over the streusel and
top with the remaining batter, then the
remaining streusel. Ask an adult to place
the cake inside the hot oven.

Bake for 40 to 45 minutes until lightly
brown on top. Ask an adult to check for
doneness by inserting a toothpick or cake
tester into the center of the coffee cake. If
it comes out clean, the cake is done. Ask
an adult to remove the cake from the hot
oven. Let cool for 20 minutes before cutting and serving.

BREADCRUMBS

Thought to originate in Germany,
the first coffee cakes were more like
sweet breads than cakes. In fact,
the topping on this and most coffee
cakes—streusel—is the German word
for "something strewn." So, with that
in mind, just lightly put the streusel
topping over your cake batter—no
need to press it in. You want it to be
nice and crumbly once it comes out of
the oven.

Chocolate Chip Cookies

12 to 18 cookies, depending on size

1 cup (2 sticks; 226 g) butter, at room temperature

¼ cup plus 2 heaping teaspoons (60 g) granulated sugar

¾ cup plus 1 tablespoon (180 g) light brown sugar

1 large egg

1 tablespoon (13 g) vanilla extract

1 cup (260 g) sourdough starter discard (see page 32)

1 cup (125 g) unbleached all-purpose flour

1 cup plus 1 teaspoon (125 g) whole wheat, whole grain flour

1 teaspoon (6 g) salt

1¼ teaspoons (5 g) baking soda

1 cup (175 g) chocolate chips

Chocolate chip cookies are a universally loved treat. Using sourdough starter discard in a cookie recipe makes the final product so tender and soft. Here, I replace half the all-purpose flour with whole wheat, whole grain flour to sneak more nutrients into this treat—and nobody notices any difference. That's my little secret. I make this recipe weekly to spoil my family with a delicious dessert, and my kids love being involved in the process.

Ask an adult to set up a stand mixer fitted with the paddle attachment. Add the butter, granulated sugar, and brown sugar to the bowl and mix on medium speed until the butter and sugars become lighter and airier. Stop the mixer and scrape down the sides of the bowl, then continue mixing for about 10 minutes.

Add the egg and vanilla and mix for 2 minutes more.

Add the sourdough starter discard and mix until well incorporated.

In a medium-size bowl, stir together the flour, salt, and baking soda. Slowly pour the dry ingredients into the batter. Mix, stopping occasionally to scrape down the sides of a bowl, until the ingredients are well incorporated. Add the chocolate chips and mix briefly to incorporate.

Patience
Transfer the bowl with the dough to the refrigerator to chill for 15 minutes.

Fun Part
Ask an adult to preheat the oven to 350°F (180°C). Line a baking sheet with parchment paper.

Using an ice cream scoop or two spoons, drop heaping tablespoons of dough onto the prepared baking sheet, 1 to 2 inches (2.5 to 5 cm) apart.

Ask an adult to place the baking sheet into the hot oven. Bake for 14 to 16 minutes until the edges of the cookies turn golden brown but the center remains lighter. Ask an adult to remove the hot baking sheet from the oven. Let the cookies cool a bit before removing them from the baking sheet. Enjoy.

BREADCRUMBS

The original chocolate chip cookies were super-crispy and the perfect size to pop into your mouth one at a time. Fast-forward to 2003, when the Immaculate Baking Company in Flat Rock, North Carolina, baked the world's largest cookie: 40,000 pounds—that's 20 tons (or 18 metric tons) with a 102-foot (31 m) diameter!

Sample Schedule

About 1 hour stands between you and these delicious cookies.

	DAY 1
Mix ingredients and refrigerate	2:00 p.m.
Scoop and bake	2:15 p.m.

BREADCRUMBS

You may have noticed that there are different types of chocolate: white, milk, and dark. And dark chocolate can be broken down even further into semisweet, bittersweet, and baking chocolate. So what's the difference? The amount of cacao present and whether it's been mixed with any other ingredients, such as milk or sugar. The darker the chocolate, the more pure cacao it has and the more bitter it will be.

Chocolate-Cherry Brownies

4 to 6 brownies

8 tablespoons (1 stick; 113 g) butter, plus more for coating the pan

¾ cup (130 g) chocolate chips

2 large eggs

½ teaspoon (3 g) salt

1 cup (200 g) sugar

½ cup (50 g) cocoa powder

1 teaspoon (4.3 g) vanilla extract

½ cup plus 1 tablespoon plus ¾ teaspoon (150 g) sourdough starter discard (see page 32)

½ (8-ounce, or 142 g) jar tart cherries in syrup or maraschino cherries, drained

Vanilla ice cream, for serving

Imagine regular brownies—so chocolatey, chewy, melt-in-your-mouth delicious. Now imagine adding a twist of additional flavor to them. For example, dried or maraschino cherries. This sounds heavenly to me. The sourdough starter discard in this recipe makes these brownies especially delicious.

Ask an adult to preheat the oven to 325°F (170°C). Coat an 8 × 8-inch (20 × 20 cm) baking dish with butter and line the dish with parchment paper.

In a medium-size microwave-safe bowl, combine the butter and chocolate chips. Ask an adult to help you microwave it on high power for 1 to 2 minutes until melted. Stir well.

Ask an adult to set up a stand mixer fitted with the paddle attachment. Pour the melted chocolate and butter into the bowl and add the eggs, salt, sugar, cocoa powder, vanilla, sourdough starter discard, and cherries. Mix on low speed for 2 to 3 minutes until well combined. Pour the batter into the prepared baking dish.

Ask an adult to place the baking dish into the hot oven. Bake for 40 to 45 minutes. Ask an adult to check for doneness by inserting a toothpick into the center of the brownies. If it comes out slightly covered in chocolate, the brownies are ready. Ask an adult to remove the hot dish from the oven. Let the brownies cool for 30 minutes before cutting into 4 to 6 squares.

Enjoy with a scoop of vanilla ice cream on top.

Sample Schedule
There are no long stretches of time required for this recipe.

YEAST BAKED GOODS

• • • •

If you don't have a lot of time to devote to baking, or if you are just getting into bread baking and want to have an easy start, this chapter is for you. Baked goods made with yeast are super-fast and super-easy. In this chapter, I share the best recipes that can be made with yeast.

Cheesy Pull-Apart
Bread with Garlic Butter
page 131

No-Knead Crusty Bread

12 slices

This is the easiest and fastest bread you will ever make. The addition of *poolish* and a small amount of rye flour results in a deep taste and aroma. Poolish is a simple mixture made of one part flour and one part water (by weight) with a tiny amount of leavening agent (yeast). It ferments for a longer time (10 to 12 hours) but adds incredible flavor to your loaf. Prepare the poolish the night before, or 12 hours ahead.

POOLISH
Bread flour:
1 cup | 120 grams

Filtered water:
½ cup | 120 grams

Active dry yeast:
Scant ⅛ teaspoon I
0.5 grams

DOUGH
1 recipe poolish

2 cups plus 1 tablespoon plus 1 teaspoon (250 g) bread flour, plus more for dusting

3¾ tablespoons (30 g) rye flour

⅔ cup (175 g) filtered water

1⅓ teaspoons (8 g) salt

Scant ⅛ teaspoon (0.5 g) active dry yeast

To make the poolish: In a medium-size bowl, stir together the bread flour, water, and yeast. Cover the bowl with plastic wrap and let ferment at room temperature (72°F to 76°F [22°C to 24.5°C]) overnight, or for 10 to 12 hours. The mixture should become bubbly.

To make the main dough: In a large bowl, combine the poolish with the remaining dough ingredients until well combined. The dough will be sticky and hard to stir after a while. Use your muscles! Cover the bowl and let autolyse (see page 38) for 1 hour. The dough will look lumpy.

Wet your hands with water and do the first stretch and fold (see page 40). Re-cover the bowl and let rest for 30 minutes in a warm place, with the preferred temperature being between 74°F and 80°F (23°C and 27°C).

Perform another stretch and fold. With each stretch, the dough will become smoother. Cover and let rest, untouched, in a warm place for 45 minutes. The dough should become full of air, puffy, and bigger. If the dough is not puffy and bigger, perform one more stretch and fold and let the dough rest for 30 minutes more.

Note: If it's too cold in your house, use your oven with the light on as a proofing chamber.

Dust a work surface with bread flour and dump the dough onto it. Preshape the dough (see page 43) and let rest, uncovered, for 20 minutes.

Patience
Shape the dough (see page 44) and transfer it to a proofing basket. Cover the dough and let rest for 1 hour.

Ask an adult to place a Dutch oven inside the oven and preheat the oven to 500°F (250°C). Let the oven heat for 45 minutes to 1 hour.

When the oven is hot, ask an adult to remove the hot pot from the oven. Flip the dough onto a piece of parchment paper. Ask an adult to score the loaf and transfer it to the hot Dutch oven.

CONTINUED

Have your adult helper place the lid on the Dutch oven and put it into the hot oven. Bake the dough for 15 minutes. Ask an adult to remove the hot lid and lower the oven temperature to 450°F (230°C). Bake the dough for 20 minutes more until golden brown. Ask an adult to remove the hot pot oven from the oven and then use the parchment paper to lift the loaf out of the hot Dutch oven and place it on a cooling rack.

Let the loaf cool for 1 to 2 hours before enjoying a slice.

Sample Schedule

After preparing the poolish the night before baking, you'll need about 5 hours to finish this recipe.

	DAY 1	DAY 2
Make the poolish	Evening	
Mix the ingredients together and autolyse		10:00 a.m.
Stretch/fold 1		11:00 a.m.
Stretch/fold 2 and proof*		11:30 a.m.
Preshape		12:15 p.m.
Shape and proof		12:35 p.m.
Preheat the oven and Dutch oven		12:50 p.m.
Bake		1:35 p.m.

*If, after the second stretch and fold, your dough is not yet puffy and bigger, perform an additional stretch and fold before proofing.

CHEESY PULL-APART BREAD WITH GARLIC BUTTER

8 tablespoons (1 stick; 120 g) butter

3 medium-size garlic cloves, minced

1 to 2 tablespoons (4 g) chopped fresh parsley (optional)

1 tablespoon (6 g) chopped scallion, white and green parts (optional)

1 teaspoon (6 g) salt

1 loaf No-Knead Crusty Bread (page 129)

1 cup (115 g) shredded mozzarella cheese

With an adult's help, in a medium-size saucepan over medium heat, melt the butter. Stir in the garlic, parsley (if using), scallion (if using), and salt until well combined.

Ask an adult to preheat the oven 350°F (180°C).

Ask an adult to help you cut the baked loaf into small cubes, but don't cut all the way through the bottom of the loaf. The bottom will hold the loaf together. Slightly open each cut and drizzle the garlic butter into the cuts. Sprinkle the mozzarella cheese over the top of the loaf. If you have leftover garlic butter, brush it all over the crust. Wrap the loaf in aluminum foil and place it on a baking sheet.

Ask an adult to put the baking sheet into the hot oven. Bake the bread for 15 to 20 minutes until the cheese is melted and the bread is warmed through. Ask an adult to remove the hot loaf from the oven. Carefully open the aluminum foil away from your face (it will let out hot steam!). Serve hot.

BREADCRUMBS

One combine harvester, a large tractor-like machine that performs multiple functions, can cut enough wheat in 9 seconds to make about 70 loaves of bread.

Pretzel Bites

24 to 36 bites

PRETZEL BITES
Scant ¾ teaspoon (2 g)
active dry yeast

½ cup plus 3 tablespoons
(165 g) lukewarm (100°F or
38°C) filtered water

2½ cups (300 g) bread flour

2½ tablespoons
(30 g) sugar

1 teaspoon (6 g) salt

1 scant teaspoon
(6 g) honey

2 tablespoons (30 g) butter,
at room temperature

Neutral oil, for the
baking sheet

BOILING
1 gallon (3.8 L) water

3 tablespoons (45 g)
baking soda

GARNISH
Sea salt (optional)

Melted butter, for brushing
the baked pretzels
(optional)

I should warn you that this recipe is addicting. This is the perfect snack, either for everyday or special occasions. It's a crowd favorite.

To make the pretzel bites: Ask an adult to set up a stand mixer fitted with the dough hook attachment. In the mixer's bowl, dissolve the yeast in the lukewarm water. Add the flour, sugar, salt, and honey. Mix the dough for 5 to 10 minutes until well incorporated. Add the butter and mix for about 2 minutes until a smooth dough develops. Cover the bowl and let rise for 2 to 3 hours at room temperature until the dough becomes lighter and almost doubles in volume. Perform a couple of stretches and folds (see page 40) every 45 minutes.

Line a baking sheet with parchment paper and generously coat it with oil.

Fun Part
Place the dough on a nonfloured surface and flatten the dough into a rectangle. Divide the dough into 4 equal pieces, about 4 ounces (115 g) each. Preshape them into 1-inch (2.5 cm)-thick cylinders, then roll each cylinder into an 8-inch (20 cm)-long rope.

Patience
Set the pretzel ropes on the prepared baking sheet. Cover and let the ropes proof for about 30 minutes in a warm (75°F, or 24°C) place until they become puffy.

Note: If you do not have a warm enough spot, use the oven with the light on as a proofing chamber.

Move the proofed pretzel ropes into the refrigerator for 30 minutes (this will help transfer them easily into boiling water).

To prepare for boiling: While the dough chills, ask a parent or other trusted adult to help you fill a large pot with the water and bring the water to a boil. Whisk in the baking soda until it dissolves.

Ask an adult to preheat the oven to 425°F (220°C). Line a baking sheet with parchment paper and generously coat it with oil.

Remove the pretzel ropes from the refrigerator. With an adult's help, put 2 ropes into the boiling water and wait for them to float to the surface (10 seconds or less). Cook for 20 to 30 seconds per side for a thin crust. Using a slotted spoon, carefully remove the pretzel ropes from the boiling water and place them on the prepared baking sheet. Let the pretzel ropes cool for 2 to 4 minutes.

CONTINUED

Fun Part

Use kitchen scissors to cut the ropes into bite-size pieces (about 1 inch, or 2.5 cm, thick). Ensure that the pretzel bites remain on the oiled parchment paper.

To garnish the pretzel bites: Sprinkle them with sea salt (if using).

Ask an adult to place the baking sheet in the hot oven. Bake the pretzels for 14 to 16 minutes until they are golden brown. Ask an adult to remove the pretzel bites from the hot oven. Brush them with melted butter (if using) while still hot for more flavor. Enjoy your pretzel bites.

Sample Schedule

You will need about 3½ hours to complete this recipe.

	DAY 1
Mix the ingredients and let rest	11:00 a.m.
Stretch/fold 1	11:45 a.m.
Stretch/fold 2	12:30 p.m.
Shape and proof	1:00 p.m.
Refrigerate	1:30 p.m.
Boil and bake	2:00 p.m.

* DELICIOUS IDEAS *

As a twist on pretzel bites, try franks in a blanket. After the dough is proofed, roll it out and cut it into strips about the width and length of a mini hot dog. Roll mini dogs in the dough. The dough will be wrapped around the hot dog twice. Cut off any excess dough. Place the wrapped dogs on a lightly oiled baking sheet and continue with the steps for boiling and baking as written.

8 bagels

Bagels

DOUGH
Scant ¾ teaspoon (2 g) active dry yeast

1 cup plus 3 tablespoons plus 1 teaspoon (290 g) filtered water

1 tablespoon plus 1 teaspoon (15 g) granulated sugar

Scant 1 teaspoon (5 g) honey

1½ teaspoons (9 g) salt

4 cups (500 g) unbleached all-purpose flour, plus more for dusting

Neutral oil, for the baking sheet

FLAVORS (OPTIONAL)
½ cup (75 g) fresh blueberries

1 teaspoon (2.3 g) ground cinnamon

½ cup (73 g) raisins

½ cup (88 g) chocolate chips

TOPPINGS (OPTIONAL)
Seeds of choice (caraway, flax, poppy, sesame)

½ cup (58 g) shredded Cheddar cheese

BOILING
1 gallon (3.8 L) water

2 tablespoons (28 g) light brown sugar

2 tablespoons (30 g) baking soda

Who doesn't like bagels? They're one of the most common breakfast foods. Bagels can be made plain or with seeds, whole grains, blueberries, chocolate chips, cinnamon and raisins, or cheesy toppings. My kids love plain bagels that they then dip into hot chocolate. The options are endless, and they're very easy to make.

To make the dough: In a small bowl, dissolve the yeast in the filtered water. Ask an adult to set up a stand mixer fitted with the dough hook attachment. Pour all the ingredients for the dough into the bowl and mix on medium speed for 5 to 10 minutes until the dough comes together in one mass. If you need to, you can finish by kneading the dough by hand on a work surface.

To add the flavors: At the end of the dough mixing stage, add the flavors (blueberries; cinnamon and raisins; or chocolate chips; if using) and mix until combined. Cover the bowl with plastic wrap and let the dough proof for 2 hours in a warm (75°F, or 24°C) place until it doubles in size and becomes puffy.

Dust a work surface with flour and dump the dough onto it. Ask a parent to use a scraper or bench knife to divide the dough into 8 equal portions. Round each piece of dough by pinching all the sides into the center (see page 44). Turn the dough upside down, with the pinched part on the bottom and the smooth part on top. Cover each ball with plastic wrap and leave the balls on the work surface for 10 to 20 minutes.

Fun Part
To shape the bagels: Line a baking sheet with parchment paper.

With your thumb, push through the center of a dough ball until you rip through it. Use your fingers to stretch a small circle into the middle of the dough ball. Place each bagel on the prepared baking sheet. Cover the bagels with plastic wrap and let proof for 1 to 1½ hours. Then, refrigerate the dough for 6 hours, or overnight.

Next Day
To make the toppings: Remove the bagels from the refrigerator and let them sit at room temperature for 1 hour.

Spread your topping of choice in a large shallow bowl or on a sheet pan.

To boil the bagels: Ask a parent or other trusted adult to help you fill a large pot with water and bring the water to a boil. Stir in the brown sugar and baking soda until dissolved.

CONTINUED

Ask an adult to preheat the oven to 425°F (220°C). Line 2 baking sheets with parchment paper and generously coat the parchment with oil. Place a third piece of parchment paper on a heatproof work surface.

Ask an adult to carefully drop 2 bagels into the boiling water.

Observe
What happens while the bagels are in the boiling water? First, you may see the bagels sink underwater. If they do sink, in 10 to 20 seconds, they will start to float to the surface. Here, yeast eats sugar from the dough and flour and exhales carbon dioxide (CO_2). Gas makes our bagels puffy and proofed and helps them float to the surface. If your bagels do not sink, that's great! They were proofed just right.

Let the bagels boil for 30 seconds, then ask an adult to flip them and boil the other side for 20 seconds. With an adult helping, use tongs to carefully remove the bagels from the boiling water and transfer to the non-oiled parchment paper to cool. Repeat with the remaining bagels.

Dip the cooled bagels into the toppings, pressing gently to adhere the toppings to the bagel, then transfer to the oiled baking sheets, topping-side up, placing them 2 to 3 inches (5 to 7.5 cm) apart.

Ask an adult to put the baking sheets with the bagels into the hot oven. Bake for 20 to 25 minutes until golden brown. Ask an adult to remove the bagels from the hot oven and let cool for 30 to 40 minutes.

Sample Schedule
You'll need 4 hours on Day 1 to make the bagels plus about 2½ hours on Day 2 to finish them.

	DAY 1	DAY 2
Mix dough ingredients	11:00 a.m.	
Proof	11:10 a.m.	
Divide and round dough	1:10 p.m.	
Shape and proof	1:30 p.m.	
Refrigerate	3:00 p.m.	
Bring to room temperature		7:00 a.m.
Boil and bake		8:00 a.m.

+ Tip
After the bagels cool, store them in a plastic bag and keep refrigerated for up to 2 weeks, or freeze for up to 2 months.

BREADCRUMBS

Did you know that bagels have been to space? In 2008, astronaut Greg Chamitoff brought eighteen bagels from a shop owned by his aunt for his fourteen-day flight in space.

BAGELS WITH CHOCOLATE-HAZELNUT SPREAD AND STRAWBERRIES

Bagels

Chocolate-hazelnut spread

Thickly sliced fresh strawberries

Ask an adult to halve the bagels lengthwise. Toast them, if you wish. Spread a generous amount of chocolate-hazelnut spread on each bagel half and top with strawberry slices. Put two halves together like a sandwich and cut it in half through the middle.

Naan

← Naan Caprese with Mozzarella and Tomatoes page 140

14 naan rounds

1 cup (240 g) lukewarm (100°F or 38°C) filtered water

3 tablespoons (45 g) milk

1 heaping teaspoon (3 g) active dry yeast

3 tablespoons plus 2 teaspoons (45 g) sugar

1 large egg

2 teaspoons (12 g) salt

4¾ cups plus 2 tablespoons (585 g) bread flour, plus more for dusting

Neutral oil, for the bowl

4 tablespoons (½ stick; 56 g) butter, melted

3 garlic cloves, minced

Well known in India, naan is a great substitute for regular bread. It can be paired with meat or salad, used as a flatbread, or even as a base for pizza. I usually make naan during summertime on the grill, but it can also be cooked on the stovetop during winter. My kids love when I make naan for lunch. Let's bake naan together.

In a large bowl, combine the lukewarm water and milk. Dissolve the yeast in the liquid. Whisk in the sugar, egg, and salt to combine.

Add half the flour and whisk to combine. Add the remaining flour and continue to whisk until well combined—you may want to switch to a rubber spatula or even use your hands for this.

Fun Part
Now, you can mix and knead the dough with your bare hands. You can work with the dough in the bowl or on a floured work surface until all the ingredients are mixed in well, 5 to 7 minutes. Try to round the dough.

Coat a large bowl with oil to prevent sticking and place the kneaded dough in it. Cover the bowl with plastic wrap and let the dough proof for 2 to 3 hours in a warm (75°F, or 24°C) place until almost doubled in volume.

Patience
Let the dough rise and double in volume.

Sprinkle a baking sheet with flour. Dust a work surface with flour and dump the dough onto it. Divide the dough into 14 small pieces and roll each piece into a 1- to 2-inch (2.5 to 5 cm) ball. Place the dough balls on the prepared baking sheet, cover with plastic wrap, and let rest for 30 minutes.

Meanwhile, in a small bowl, stir together the melted butter and garlic.

Ask an adult to place a skillet on the stovetop over medium heat until hot. Using a rolling pin, roll each dough ball into a thin circle. Have a trusted adult help you put the dough into the hot skillet. Cook for 2 to 3 minutes. With a spatula, flip the naan to the other side. Cook for 2 minutes more until you see brown spots on each side. With an adult helping, carefully remove the naan from the skillet and place it on a plate. Using a pastry brush, spread the garlic butter on each side of the naan. Repeat the process with the remaining dough balls. Serve immediately.

CONTINUED

BREADCRUMBS

Developed about 2,500 years ago in India, naan was created as an experiment after the arrival of yeast from Egypt.

Sample Schedule

You will need about 4 hours to complete this recipe.

	DAY 1
Mix the ingredients, knead, and proof	8:00 a.m.
Divide and round dough	10:00 a.m.
Divide and roll dough	11:00 a.m.
Cook	11:30 a.m.

* DELICIOUS IDEAS *

NAAN CAPRESE WITH MOZZARELLA AND TOMATOES

4 cooked naans (page 139)

½ cup (123 g) tomato sauce

8 ounces (225 g) fresh mozzarella, cut or torn into chunks

½ cup (75 g) cherry tomatoes, halved

Salt

12 to 16 fresh basil leaves

4 teaspoons (21 g) balsamic vinegar

Ask an adult to preheat the oven to 375°F (190°C).

Place the naan on a baking sheet. Top each naan with 2 tablespoons (30 g) of tomato sauce. Sprinkle chunks of mozzarella and tomato halves over the naan.

Ask an adult to put the baking sheet into the hot oven. Bake the naan pizzas for 5 to 7 minutes until the cheese melts and the crust is golden. Ask an adult to remove the pizzas from the hot oven and sprinkle them with salt to taste. Garnish the naan with basil leaves, then drizzle each with 1 teaspoon of vinegar. Serve hot.

* * *

NAAN PIZZA ROLL

Spread pizza sauce and sprinkle shredded mozzarella cheese over the cooked naan. Ask a parent or other trusted adult to preheat the broiler. Ask an adult to put the pizzas under the broiler. Cook for 10 minutes, watching carefully, until the cheese melts. Ask an adult to remove the pizzas from the oven and let cool for a couple of minutes. Shape the naan into a roll and cut into smaller pieces to serve.

Super-Soft Milk Buns

9 buns

7 tablespoons
plus 2 teaspoons
(115 g) lukewarm (100°F
or 38°C) milk

Scant ¾ teaspoon (2 g)
active dry yeast

2½ cups (300 g) bread flour

2 tablespoons plus
2 teaspoons (50 g)
sweetened condensed milk

1 large egg, at room
temperature

2½ tablespoons
(30 g) sugar

Scant 1 teaspoon (5 g) salt

3 tablespoons plus
1 teaspoon (50 g) butter,
at room temperature, plus
2 tablespoons (28 g) butter,
melted (optional)

These milk buns are perfect for breakfast, served with butter, jam, or chocolate-hazelnut spread. They also do great as a dinner roll replacement. The rolls can stay fresh for up to three days. I prefer to use a smaller amount of yeast and a longer fermentation time when I make these buns. It helps eliminate the strong yeast flavor.

Ask an adult to set up a stand mixer fitted with the dough hook attachment. In the bowl, stir together the lukewarm milk and yeast until the yeast dissolves. Add the flour, sweetened condensed milk, egg, sugar, and salt. Mix the dough on medium speed for 2 to 3 minutes. The dough will look stiff at the beginning.

Add the room-temperature butter and increase the speed to medium-high. Mix the dough until the butter is combined, stopping to scrape down the sides with a spatula, as needed. Continue mixing for about 15 minutes, stopping to scrape down the sides, as needed: the dough will become softer and smoother and, eventually, come together and appear shiny.

Perform a windowpane test (see page 38) to double-check whether the gluten developed properly. If it hasn't, keep mixing until you get a good windowpane.

Patience
Cover the dough and put it in a warm (75°F, or 24°C) place to proof for 2 to 3 hours, or in the oven with the light on. During that time, perform 2 stretches and folds (see page 40) every 45 minutes. The dough should become puffy and almost double in volume.

Line an 8 × 8-inch (20 × 20 cm) ovenproof baking dish with parchment paper.

Dump the dough onto a nonfloured work surface and divide it into 9 equal pieces.

Fun Part
Shape each piece of dough by simply folding the edges into the middle to form a small pouch. Place the dough balls, seam-side down, on your work surface. Cup your hand over a dough ball and lightly roll it into a ball, using the friction of the work surface to help with the rounding. Repeat with all the dough balls. Transfer the rolls to the prepared baking dish.

Patience
Cover the rolls and let proof in a warm (75°F, or 24°C) place for 1 to 2 hours until they double in volume.

CONTINUED

Note: If you need a warm place, use the oven with the light on as a proofing chamber.

Ask an adult to preheat the oven to 375°F (190°C).

Uncover the rolls and ask an adult to put them into the hot oven. Sprinkle proofed rolls with flour (optional).

Bake the rolls for 22 to 25 minutes until golden brown. Ask an adult to remove the hot rolls from the hot oven. Let the rolls cool completely.

Note: To add more shine and extra softness to the crust, you may brush the still-hot rolls with melted butter.

Sample Schedule
You will need just under 4 hours to complete this recipe.

	DAY 1
Mix ingredients	12:00 p.m.
Windowpane test and proof	12:15 p.m.
Stretch/fold 1	1:00 p.m.
Stretch/fold 2	1:45 p.m.
Divide dough and proof	2:15 p.m.
Bake	3:15 p.m.

* DELICIOUS IDEAS *

CHEESY EGG BREAKFAST ROLL

8 Super-Soft Milk Buns (page 141), split horizontally

16 slices yellow cheese

4 large eggs, scrambled to your liking

3 tablespoons plus 1 teaspoon (47 g) butter, melted

Ask an adult to preheat the oven to 350°F (180°C). Line a baking sheet with parchment paper.

Arrange the rolls, cut-side up, on the prepared baking sheet. Place 1 slice of cheese on each bottom roll. Top the cheese with scrambled eggs. Place another slice of cheese on top of the eggs. Cover the eggs with the top roll. Brush the rolls with melted butter.

Ask an adult to put the baking sheet into the oven. Bake the rolls for 20 minutes until the cheese is fully melted and everything is warmed through.

* * *

PERFECT PB&J

Spread your favorite nut or seed butter and jam on the roll and enjoy as a quick snack or light lunch.

Chocolate Babka

10 to 12 slices

DOUGH

¼ cup plus 2 teaspoons (70 g) lukewarm (100°F or 38°C) whole milk

Scant ¾ teaspoon to 1 heaping teaspoon (2 to 3 g) active dry yeast

¼ cup plus 2 teaspoons (60 g) sugar

2 large eggs, at room temperature

Scant 1 teaspoon (5 g) salt

2½ cups (300 g) bread flour

3 tablespoons plus 1 teaspoon (50 g) butter, at room temperature

FILLING

½ cup (130 g) chocolate-hazelnut spread

EGG WASH

1 large egg

2 tablespoons (30 g) water

¼ teaspoon (1.5 g) salt

The dough of this chocolate babka is so unique; it has a soft, rich flavor that can be used not only for chocolate babka, but also for babka made with jam, cinnamon, apples, or even pistachio filling (see page 147).

To make the dough: Ask an adult to set up a stand mixer fitted with the dough hook attachment. In the bowl, stir together the lukewarm milk and yeast until the yeast dissolves. Add the sugar, eggs, and salt. Mix well with a spoon, then add the flour. Mix the dough on medium speed for 1 to 2 minutes until the ingredients are well incorporated.

Increase the speed to medium-high and mix the dough for 3 to 5 minutes until it starts to come together in a single mass. It will clear the bowl, but still stick to the bottom.

Note: Mixing until the dough comes together is a very important step, as it develops the gluten, so it can hold the butter.

Add the butter and mix on medium-high speed for 10 to 15 minutes until the dough comes together and doesn't stick to the bottom of the bowl, stopping occasionally to scrape down the sides of the bowl with a spatula.

Perform a windowpane test (see page 38).

Patience

Cover the dough and let proof for 2 to 3 hours in a warm (75°F, or 24°C) place, or use the oven with the light on as a proofing chamber.

During that time, perform 2 stretches and folds (see page 40) every 45 minutes. The dough should become puffy and airy, and double in volume.

Dump the dough onto a nonfloured work surface.

Fun Part

To fill the dough: Line a baking sheet with parchment paper and line a 9 × 5-inch (23 × 13 cm) loaf pan with parchment.

Using a rolling pin, roll the dough into an 8 × 16 inch (20 × 40 cm) rectangle, ¼ inch (6 mm) thick. Spread the filling over the dough all the way to the edges. Starting with a long side closest to you, roll the dough into a tight roll. Transfer the roll to the prepared baking sheet, seam-side down. Move the sheet to the freezer for 10 minutes.

Note: Freezing the dough will help make it easier to cut.

Ask an adult to help you halve the dough lengthwise, so the filling is exposed. Braid the halves together and place the loaf into the prepared loaf pan. If your braid is longer than the pan, fold the ends of the dough under as you place it in the loaf pan. Cover the pan with plastic wrap.

Patience
Let the dough proof for 2 hours in a warm (75°F, or 24°C) place until it doubles, or more, in volume.

Ask an adult to preheat the oven to 375°F (190°C).

While the oven heats, make the egg wash: In a small bowl, whisk the egg, water, and salt to blend. Use a pastry brush to brush the egg wash on top of the babka.

Ask an adult to place the loaf pan in the hot oven. Bake the babka for 30 to 35 minutes until golden brown. Ask an adult to remove the hot babka from the hot oven. Let cool for 1 hour. Remove from the pan and enjoy.

Sample Schedule
You'll need about 6 hours to make the babka.

	DAY 1
Mix ingredients	12:00 p.m.
Proof	12:30 p.m.
Stretch/fold 1	1:15 p.m.
Stretch/fold 2	2:00 p.m.
Roll dough, add filling, and freeze	2:45 p.m.
Cut, braid, and proof	2:55 p.m.
Bake	4:55 p.m.

APPLE CINNAMON BABKA

1 tablespoon (14 g) butter

2 large apples, washed and cut into thin slices

⅔ cup (150 g) light brown sugar

2 scant tablespoons (15 g) unbleached all-purpose flour

1 tablespoon (7 g) ground cinnamon

¼ teaspoon (1.5 g) salt

1 large egg white

With an adult's help, in a saucepan over medium heat, melt the butter. Add the apples and cook, stirring, for about 3 minutes until slightly softened. Remove from the heat.

In a small bowl, stir together the remaining ingredients until they form a paste. Spread the cinnamon paste over the dough, instead of the chocolate-hazelnut spread, and top with the softened apples.

Finish the recipe as instructed.

* * *

PISTACHIO BABKA

4 tablespoons (½ stick; 56 g) butter, at room temperature

¼ cup (50 g) sugar

1 large egg white

½ teaspoon (2 g) almond extract

1 teaspoon (4.3 g) vanilla extract

½ cup (65 g) finely ground unsalted pistachios or pistachio flour

1 tablespoon (7.8 g) unbleached all-purpose flour

In a small bowl, stir together the butter and sugar until incorporated. Add the egg white, almond extract, and vanilla and mix well. Add the pistachio flour and the all-purpose flour and stir to combine.

Use the pistachio spread instead of the chocolate-hazelnut spread and finish the recipe as directed.

Doughnuts

12 medium-size ring doughnuts

Doughnuts are universally loved. These delicious doughnuts are soft as a cloud, with an amazing melt-in-your-mouth texture. This is the best recipe you can get.

DOUGH
½ cup plus 2 tablespoons (150 g) lukewarm (100°F or 38°C) milk

Scant ¾ teaspoon (2 g) active dry yeast

2½ tablespoons (30 g) granulated sugar

1 teaspoon (6 g) salt

1 large egg

1 large egg yolk

2⅔ cups (330 g) unbleached all-purpose flour, plus 2 scant tablespoons (15 g), as needed, plus more for dusting

4 tablespoons (½ stick; 56 g) butter, at room temperature

FRYING
1 quart (946 ml) neutral oil

To make the dough: Ask an adult to set up a stand mixer fitted with the dough hook attachment. In the bowl, stir together the lukewarm milk and yeast until the yeast dissolves. Add the granulated sugar, salt, egg, and egg yolk and mix well with spoon. Add the 2⅔ cups (330 g) of flour. Mix the dough on medium speed for 1 to 2 minutes until well incorporated.

Increase the speed to medium-high and mix the dough for 3 to 5 minutes until the dough starts to come together. It will release from the sides but will still stick to the bottom of the bowl.

Note: Mixing until the dough comes together is a very important step, as it develops the gluten, so it can hold the butter.

Add the butter and mix on medium-high speed for 10 to 15 minutes until the dough comes together and doesn't stick to the bottom of the bowl, stopping occasionally to scrape down the sides of the bowl with a spatula.

Note: There should be no dough sticking to the mixing bowl. If the dough is too sticky, add the remaining 1 to scant 2 tablespoons (7.8 to 15 g) of flour and continue mixing.

Perform a windowpane test (see page 38).

Patience
Cover the dough and let proof for 2 hours in a warm (75°F, or 24°C) place, or use the oven with a light on as a proofing chamber.

During that time, perform 1 stretch and fold (see page 40). The dough should become puffy and airy, and double in volume.

If you're going to glaze or ice your dough-nuts, you can also make those toppings during this time.

CONTINUED

GLAZE (OPTIONAL)
2 cups (240 g) powdered sugar

¼ cup (60 g) hot water

½ teaspoon (2 g) vanilla extract

VANILLA ICING (OPTIONAL)
1½ cups (180 g) powdered sugar

2 tablespoons (30 g) whole milk

1 teaspoon (4.3 g) vanilla extract

CHOCOLATE ICING (OPTIONAL)
1 cup (175 g) chocolate chips

4 tablespoons (½ stick; 56 g) butter

4 teaspoons (27 g) honey

4 teaspoons (20 g) water

To make the glaze (if using): In a medium microwave-safe bowl, whisk the glaze ingredients until blended and smooth. Set aside. If the glaze hardens, microwave it on high power for 5 to 10 seconds, then give it a stir.

To make the vanilla icing (if using): In a medium microwave-safe bowl, whisk the vanilla icing ingredients until blended and smooth. Set aside. If the icing hardens, microwave it on high power for 5 to 10 seconds, then give it a stir.

To make the chocolate icing (if using): In a medium microwave-safe bowl, combine the chocolate icing ingredients. Ask an adult to microwave it on high power for 20 seconds. Stir the icing and microwave for a couple more seconds, or until the icing is melted and smooth. Set aside. If the icing hardens, microwave it on high power for 5 to 10 seconds, then give it a stir.

Fun Part
Line a baking sheet with parchment paper.

Dust a work surface with flour and dump the dough onto it. Using a rolling pin, gently roll the dough to ½-inch (1 cm) thickness.

Using a floured doughnut cutter, cut out about 12 doughnuts and place them on the prepared baking sheet.

Note: Once you can't possibly cut any more doughnuts, gather the scraps into a mass, reroll the dough, and cut more doughnuts.

Patience
Loosely cover the doughnuts with plastic wrap and let rise for about 1 hour in a warm (75°F, or 24° C) place until they become puffier.

Thirty minutes before the proofing ends, ask an adult to help you pour the oil into a large heavy skillet over medium heat. Let the oil heat to 350°F (180°C) on a deep-frying thermometer. Line a wire rack with paper towels.

Under strict adult supervision—because the oil is very hot and may burn you easily—using a wide spatula, carefully slide about 4 doughnuts into the hot oil. Cook for 1 minute, then flip to the other side. Cook for about 1 minute more, or until each side is golden brown. With an adult helper, carefully remove the doughnuts from the hot oil and place on the prepared wire rack to drain.

Note: If you'd like glazed doughnuts, dip them into the glaze while they are still hot and place on the wire rack, glazed-side up, to drain. If you'd like iced doughnuts, wait until they cool, then dip them into the icing. And for sugar-dusted doughnuts, let the doughnuts cool off and simply roll them in granulated sugar.

BREADCRUMBS

Did you know that more than 10 **billion** doughnuts are made in the United States each year? While pretty evenly dispersed throughout the country, Boston is the city with the most doughnut shops per person. Perhaps a fact that goes hand in hand with this statistic: It's also the city with the most Dunkin' Donuts per square mile.

Sample Schedule

You will need about 3 hours 30 minutes to make the doughnuts before frying them with an adult helper.

	DAY 1
Mix dough ingredients	7:00 a.m.
Windowpane test and proof	7:30 a.m.
Stretch/fold	8:30 a.m.
Roll dough, cut, and proof	9:30 a.m.
Heat oil	10:00 a.m.
Cook	10:30 a.m.

Resources

Tutorials & More Recipes
Natasha's Baking
www.natashasbaking.com

Breadtopia
www.breadtopia.com

Equipment
Challenger Breadware
www.challengerbreadware.com

Wire Monkey
www.wiremonkey.com

Sur la Table
www.surlatable.com

Metrics & Conversions
Aqua-Calc
www.aqua-calc.com/calculate/
food-volume-to-weight

Tablespoon
www.tablespoon.com/meals/
tablespoon-conversions

King Arthur Baking Company
www.kingarthurbaking.com/learn/
ingredient-weight-chart

Blank Sample Schedule
Baking bread takes time, patience, and planning. We provided you with sample schedules, but you can also use this blank schedule to plan out your baking days!

Day 1: _____ hours _____ minutes

Day 2: _____ hours _____ minutes

	DAY 1	DAY 2
_____		
_____		
_____		
_____		
_____		
_____		
_____		
_____		
_____		
_____		

Sources

Bulow, Alessandra. "5 Things You Didn't Know About Chocolate Chip Cookies." *Epicurious*. July 30, 2014. Epicurious.com/archive/blogs/editor/201⅝7/things-you-didnt-know-about-chocolate-chip-cookies.html.

Ehler, James T. "Poppy Seeds." Food Facts and Trivia: Poppy Seeds. FoodReference.com. Accessed March 5, 2021. FoodReference.com/html/fpoppyseeds.html.

Hopkins, John Bryan. "April 7 Is National Coffee Cake Day." *Foodimentary*. April 7, 2015. Foodimentary.com/tag/coffee-cake.

Hopkins, John Bryan. "April 10 Is National Cinnamon Roll Day." *Foodimentary*. April 10, 2015. Foodimentary.com/201⅝4⁄10/april-10-is-national-cinnamon-roll-day.

Hussein, Jennifer. "50 Mouthwatering Pizza Facts: Eat This, Not That!" *Eat This Not That*. November 5, 2020. EatThis.com/pizza-facts.

Idaho Potato Museum. "Potato Facts." Idaho Potato Museum. Accessed March 5, 2021. IdahoPotatoMuseum.com/potato-facts.

Mobile-Cuisine. "Tortilla Fun Facts: Mobile Cuisine." Mobile-Cuisine.com | Food Truck, Pop Up and Street Food Coverage, March 31, 2017. Mobile-Cuisine.com/did-you-know/tortilla-fun-facts.

Myrick, Richard. "Smore Fun Facts: Mobile Cuisine." Mobile-Cuisine.com | Food Truck, Pop Up, and Street Food Coverage. August 10, 2020. Mobile-Cuisine.com/did-you-know/smore-fun-facts.

National Confectioners Association. "Fun Facts About Chocolate." Candy USA. April 21, 2020. CandyUSA.com/story-of-chocolate/fun-facts-about-chocolate.

Selna, Elaine. "Make a Single Cup of Coffee or Tea Directly in a Mug with This Portable Brewing Tool." *Mental Floss*. February 26, 2021. MentalFloss.com/article/642865/sustainably-brew-cup-coffee-tea-finalpress-kickstarter.

SouthFloridaReporter.com. "On Average, Every American Eats 53 Pounds of Bread a Year." *South Florida Reporter*. November 17, 2018. SouthFloridaReporter.com/on-average-every-american-eats-53-pounds-of-bread-a-year.

Speake, Carol. "National Buttermilk Biscuit Day—May 14—Southern Style Biscuits Anyone?" *Always the Holidays*. May 12, 2020. AlwaystheHolidays.com/national-buttermilk-biscuit-day.

Taste for Life Magazine. "Power to the Purple . . . Corn!" tflmag.com. February 22, 2021. tflmag.com/power-to-the-purple-corn.

Velez, Adriana. "5 Weird and Wonderful Things About Butter That Will Make You Love It Even More." *CafeMom*. April 4, 2013. CafeMom.com/lifestyle/153672-5_weird_wonderful_things_about.

Westminster Cheddar. "20 Eye-Opening Cheddar Facts All Cheese Lovers Must Know!" Somerdale International. December 9, 2015. WestminsterCheddar.com/20-eye-opening-cheddar-facts.

Wikipedia. "Parable of the Leaven." Wikimedia Foundation. December 17, 2020. https://en.m.wikipedia.org/wiki/Parable_of_the_Leaven.

WPBF. "Fun Facts! National Blueberry Muffin Day." WPBF. July 13, 2017. wpbf.com/article/fun-facts-national-blueberry-muffin-day/1157212.

Appendix

Temperature and Proportions for Sourdough Starter

As discussed on page 26, ambient temperature and the proportions of ingredients put into your sourdough starter go hand in hand. If your house is warmer or cooler than the ranges discussed earlier, you may need to adjust the amount of ingredients you put into your starter as you are building it. Let's take a look at how different proportions speed up the time of fermentation at the same ambient temperature range (75°F to 80°F, or 24°C to 27°C).

Proportions by weight *	Time to Peak
1:2:2	4 hours
1:3:3	5 hours
1:4:4	6 hours
1:5:5	7 hours
1:6:6	8 hours
1:7:7	9 hours
1:8:8	10 hours

*seed starter : filtered water : flour

And let's compare how different proportions delay the fermentation of your starter at lower environment temperatures (60°F to 70°F, or 15°C to 21°C).

Proportions by weight*	Time to Peak
1:2:2	6 to 10 hours
1:3:3	10 to 12 hours
1:4:4	12 to 16 hours
1:5:5	16 to 18 hours
1:6:6	18 to 24 hours

*seed starter : filtered water : flour

To make your feedings easier, let's create a schedule, which will help you make your starter as happy as it can be.

If the temperature in your house is between 71°F and 76°F (22°C and 24.5°C), you need to do two feedings a day: one in the morning and one in the evening:

MORNING	EVENING
1:4:4 by weight	1:4:4 by weight
15 g seed starter : 60 g filtered water : 55 g bread flour + 5 g whole wheat, whole grain flour	15 g seed starter : 60 g filtered water : 55 g bread flour + 5 g whole wheat, whole grain flour

If the temperature in your house is lower, between 60°F and 70°F (15°C and 21°C), you can do just one feeding per day:

MORNING
1:6:6 by weight
15 g starter : 90 g filtered water : 80 g bread flour + 10 g whole wheat, whole grain flour

Storing Your Sourdough Starter for Future Use

Life gets busy, and sometimes we can't feed the starter or get to baking with it right away. But, here is a secret to preserving your starter, storing it properly, and keeping it alive for future use. First, feed your starter with slightly higher proportions to give more food for bacteria to survive in a colder environment. In a medium-size (10- to 12-ounce, or 300 to 360 ml) jar, mix:

	VOLUME	WEIGHT
Ripe (seed) starter	1 tablespoon	15 grams
Filtered water	4 tablespoons	60 grams
Bread flour	6 tablespoons	45 grams
Whole wheat, whole grain flour	2 tablespoons	15 grams

Loosely cover the jar with a lid to allow some air in. Let sit at room temperature for 2 hours, then transfer the jar with the starter to the refrigerator. The starter can safely stay in the refrigerator for up to 1 month.

OBSERVE

During the first 2 hours at room temperature, bacteria and wild yeast will start multiplying and growing. When moved to the refrigerator, the colder temperature will slow the fermentation process because the cooler temperature makes the bacteria and wild yeast less active—they don't want to eat as much as when they are in a warm environment. This slows food consumption, allowing the starter to stay in the refrigerator much longer without further feedings.

Bringing Your Sourdough Starter Back to Life

Once you are ready to bake and you are confident you will be able to feed your starter consistently, it's time to remove your sourdough friend from the refrigerator and wake it up. Remove your sourdough starter from the refrigerator and let it warm at room temperature for 1 to 2 hours. Remove all the ripe starter from the jar, except 1 tablespoon, or 15 g, saved for the seed. The removed starter should be discarded.

	VOLUME	WEIGHT
Ripe (seed) starter	1 tablespoon	15 grams
Filtered water	2 tablespoons	30 g
Bread flour	3 tablespoons + 1 teaspoon	25 grams
Whole wheat, whole grain flour	2 teaspoons	5 grams

Mix the seed starter with the water, bread flour, and whole wheat, whole grain flour. Let the starter ferment for 10 to 12 hours at room temperature.

OBSERVE

In the warm environment, the bacteria start to wake up and need food. When mixed with flour and water, the bacteria and microorganisms will exhale carbon dioxide (CO_2), producing bubbles, which help the starter grow. Notice how the starter is beginning to bubble and smell sour? You will also see it double or more in volume. Perform three more feedings, once every 12 hours. After the third and final feeding, your starter will become stronger and ready for baking.

Performing a Float Test

Once your starter wakes up and you've fed it three times, you want to make sure it is ready for baking. There is a simple way to figure that out—a "float test." Let's see how it works.

- After the starter is fed, let it ferment at room temperature for 4 to 6 hours.

- Fill a bowl with room-temperature water.

- Drop 1 tablespoon, or 15 g, of starter into the water.

If your starter is alive, it will float to the surface and it is ready to use for baking.

If your starter isn't ready yet, it will sink to the bottom of the bowl. When this happens, repeat the feeding process one or two more times, every 12 hours, before using the starter in a dough.

Acknowledgments

My biggest gratitude goes to all the people who made this book come to life. The process felt like a collaborative effort of growing starter, but at a different level :)

I want to thank my husband, Val, creator of my website NatashasBaking.com, for being my mentor, helper, and biggest support. He is my greatest cheerleader with any project.

My kids, Sasha and Jacob, for their help in the kitchen: We wanted to make sure that any child can use the recipes from this book, and it's been proven by my kids. Also, they were the main tasters and judges.

I want to thank the Instagram sourdough community, so full of many amazing bakers who are always willing to share their knowledge every day.

I really appreciate all of my followers and readers for your everyday support and for sharing with me the love of baking, in general, and sourdough baking, in particular.

And, of course, The Quarto Group, who reached out to me, encouraged me to write a book, and made this book a reality.

Thank you all.

Sincerely, Natalya

About the Author

Natalya Syanova is a Chicago-based mother of two and a sourdough expert with more than eight years' baking experience. In 2013, she attended Food Enthusiast classes at the French Pastry School in Chicago to understand how to bake pastries professionally from the industry's best bakers. And by 2020, her platform @NatashasBaking was named by *Forbes Online* as one of the top bread influencers that are go-to reference when you are learning to bake bread at home. She is constantly exploring chemistry methods, flour types, proofing techniques, and more—proving that beautiful bread is both a science and an art. Natalya brings the age-old secrets of successful bread baking to a new generation of bakers.

INDEX